M. Curtis McCoy

How To Be

Successful

Think Like A Leader

Contents

Preface

I've always enjoyed motivational talks, pumped up workout music, and inspirational books. Each day, I commit to doing something to improve.

In 2015 I launched "Success, Motivation & Inspiration" as a blog to motivate and inspire others to achieve more in their lives. Around the same time, I began connecting with aspiring entrepreneurs and seasoned experts. I was looking for others who wanted to increase their business and expand their market presence. I used the blog to jot down thoughts when I discovered something that inspired me.

As my social media groups gained thousands of members globally, I started receiving calls and messages from people whose lives had improved because of the principles I shared. Others reached out for guidance or advice on how to become successful.

I started spending time with successful people who were achieving improvement in their own lives. Many of these new friends had created lifestyles that allowed them to do things that others could only imagine. The more time I spent around successful friends, the more ideas and opportunities started falling into my lap. Even though I wasn't concentrating on writing or social media, interest continued to grow.

Why Did I Start Writing This Book?

One night I received a call from someone who was contemplating suicide. Desperate for hope, this individual told me they didn't know why, but they joined the Success, Motivation & Inspiration Facebook group while trying to decide if they should end their life or not. Thankfully, I got a chance to talk with them before they made a terrible decision. We talked about how they felt as if they had no chance of being anything but a failure.

That's when I began to realize this project deserved additional attention. When I launched the website a couple of years earlier, it was just a hobby. I just wanted to help prospective entrepreneurs in my free time. After this call, I decided to include real-life stories and interviews with people who chose to improve their lives. I've interviewed professional athletes, preachers, wealthy investors, inventors, expert negotiators, and even ex-convicts turned entrepreneurs.

In the following chapters, I mix these interviews with life lessons that apply to business, relationships, and all aspects of being truly successful. I hope this book will help you achieve your ambitions, motivate you never to give up, and inspire you to pursue greatness.

CHAPTER 1

Introduction

By the time I was 27 years old, I owned companies in various industries, including medical, fashion, manufacturing, distribution, and pharmaceuticals. I had become successful at a young age, and life was great!

Everything changed when I started having daily grand mal seizures. In 2010, I was diagnosed with brain cancer. Oncologists gave me only 60-90 days to live. I lost absolutely everything as I became unable to drive, live alone, or remember small details such as if I'd eaten, or taken an insulin shot. Everything I had researched, the businesses I had built, and even my memory were gone.

My family took me to Tijuana, Mexico, to pursue alternative treatments. Uncertain of whether I'd survive or not, I was inspired to make a difference in as many lives as possible.

I began contacting leaders I admired and asking questions. How To Be Successful: Think Like A Leader is a compilation of true stories & conversations that will help you in your journey to success.

Learn how to be successful! Create a life that's not only financially prosperous but also balanced and enjoyable.

CHAPTER 2

What Is Your Excuse?

A few years ago, I met a guy driving a custom twin-turbo Ferrari. I decided to introduce myself and ask how he became so successful. Surprisingly, he told me a story that's stuck with me for years. He shared that his wife left him after they lost their home. Bankrupt and living on the street, he decided that he had to do something with his life during his first night sleeping in the park.

He started visiting construction sites, trying to get a job. Many of them turned him down, but the last job site he visited mentioned a particular problem. The company that generally supplied their roofing trusses had messed up an order (again).

He told me that he'd done some construction work as a teenager. He went to a pawn shop and picked up a circular saw, combination square, tape measure, and a hammer. That night, after everyone at the construction company went home, he returned to the job site. He spent hours building "the perfect truss" to give them the next morning, using lumber he found on-site.

They were impressed with the quality, and he closed that first deal. They gave him payment in advance for the entire order, so he had money to buy the lumber and supplies he needed plus some profit. That was the start of his custom truss company and the beginning of his success.

What Is Your Excuse?

Are you working a job you hate? Do you need to make more money? Is there a business idea that could change your entire life? Are you struggling to lose some extra weight? The challenge for many people is not finding their goal but deciding to pursue it. What is your excuse for not achieving your goal?

Seeing this guy pull up in a bright yellow, twin-turbo Ferrari, many people respond with, "It must be nice!" You might assume that he was born into money, or that he was just "one of those rich guys" for most of his life. It would be easy to think he didn't know what it was like to struggle. I would never have guessed from the Ferrari he was driving, or the clothes he was wearing, that he had been homeless a few years earlier.

Create Opportunities For Success

After going bankrupt, losing his wife, and living on the street, this man decided to choose the direction of his future. He didn't sit on the side of the road with a cardboard sign asking for handouts. He started visiting construction site after construction site, in search of a job. When they denied him a position as a laborer, he found a problem the company was experiencing and created a solution. This gentleman made millions of dollars because he didn't give up when life gave him lemons.

Provide A Solution

Business ideas often fail because they don't provide a solution to a problem. If you're creating a new business, you may find success more quickly if you fill a gap in the market. If you're trying to expand an existing business, you will likely succeed by providing a solution to a problem your potential customers are already experiencing. Do some research, ask customers, and discover the "pain points" in your target industry. Discover problems. Create a solution.

Be Willing To Risk Short-Term Comfort

Although he was already homeless, this guy took the last few dollars he had and invested in himself to buy the tools to build his future. He didn't squander his last few bucks on a hotel room or a bottle of liquor; instead, he created an opportunity. By risking short-term comfort, he was able to build the foundation for a business that has made him extremely wealthy.

Imagine you are living on the street, with only a few dollars to your name. Would you spend what little you had left on tools instead of food or a place to sleep? Taking a calculated risk could be the difference between short-term comfort or a lifetime of success!

CHAPTER 3

Don't Miss Your "Orange Creamsicle"

The other day I drove past a homeless guy sitting in the shade to escape the heat of the day. As I passed, he aggressively flipped me off with pain in his eyes and yelled, "Rich f***n' prick!" because he saw me driving a Jaguar. I hadn't done anything to make him hate me except drive by in a nice car. He likely thinks that successful people were born with a silver spoon in their mouth. Did he hate me because he assumed I was "dealt better cards in life" than he received?

I don't know this guy, but he may have grown up in a bad situation. He may not know any successful people or have many positive influences in his life. He may not understand that life is what you decide to make of it. I wanted to connect with this guy and give him a bit of encouragement. Maybe I could tell him about the man I spoke with a few years earlier who had lost everything but started his own multi-million dollar company after living on the street. This other guy went from homeless to driving a twin-turbo Ferrari by deciding to create a better future.

Would it help this homeless man to share my story? I had lived in the back of my phone store for years, surviving malignant brain cancer and diabetes. I had to drive to the gym each morning because I didn't have a shower in the back of the store. Although I didn't know his exact situation, I've been down and out before, so I could sympathize. I decided to approach him.

There's Always An Opportunity To Improve

Would it help to share how I'd been fired from numerous jobs for having seizures at work? Should I tell him there's hope for a better tomorrow if he buckles down and takes responsibility for his future? I'd love to share what my mom always says:

"Work like it's up to you and pray like it's up to God."

Maybe I could give him a little hope by sharing my personal experience. What would you tell this poor guy?

Don't Miss Your Opportunity

As I thought about how to help give this guy a little hope, I realized that just dropping a bag of food wouldn't create any lasting connection. I thought if he'd let me sit down and listen to his story, I may be able to gain some insight into what made him hate "the rich prick" in the Jaguar. If we could connect as brothers, then maybe I could influence the path I'm on now. Perhaps I could help him decide to change his attitude and improve his own life.

I went home and came back with an Orange Creamsicle®, a bottle of cold water, and a V8® sparkling energy drink. When I pulled up, he was already yelling at someone else

11

in a beautiful white Mercedes. He was actively trying to start a fight, so I thought this might not be the best idea that afternoon. His negative attitude made me apprehensive about reaching out to help him. The plan was to help someone improve their life, not get into a physical altercation! I opted to drive on by and ate the Popsicle® myself.

That was a reminder to me that often, we are where we're at in life because of our choices. Our decisions, our outlook on life, and our attitude play a massive role in where we end up. If you're currently struggling in life, keep a positive outlook, and improve your situation. Don't miss your opportunity because of your negativity. Keep an open mind and a positive attitude regardless of your starting point. The cards you're dealt in life don't determine whether you'll win the game or not!

CHAPTER 4

Interview with M. Curtis McCoy

I'm an author, business owner, and keynote speaker. I write books that help readers in communication, leadership, and personal branding.

In this book, I share conversations with other leaders and entrepreneurs about success and personal growth.

Below are my answers to the questions I asked them.

What is your definition of success?

I often think of the quote from Earl Nightingale, "Success is the progressive realization of a worthwhile dream." Although I've experienced many difficulties after surviving brain cancer, I've been able to surround myself with an incredible team, and I've built some great friendships while writing this book!

Success is about doing something that improves the lives of others and makes you truly happy.

When did you consider yourself a success?

I'd like to share a quick story that made me feel pretty special. We all have secret admirers, but if you look up to someone, make an effort to let them know!

Shortly after publishing my third book, someone chased me down at the San

Francisco International Airport. They said, "I just wanted to let you know I've read all your books. You are amazing, Mr. McCoy. I'm your biggest fan!" I didn't even know I had any fans at the time.

Being asked to speak at events or being interviewed by a major publication feels nice, but being admired by a fan has more impact on me.

What steps do you take daily to improve?

For personal growth, I listen to podcasts, motivational videos, and attend success talks and seminars. I read a lot of self-improvement books and make it a point to surround myself with positive people.

To improve physically, I mountain bike, hike, or go to the gym regularly, and much of my diet consists of locally grown, organic foods.

I write or blog 5 to 6 days per week. Writing quality content requires studying and forces me to organize my thoughts and reflect on them.

For spiritual health, I strive to study the Bible daily.

What have you recognized as your greatest strengths, and how have they impacted your success?

I've always had great foresight and the ability to take advantage of opportunities that no one else sees.

I take pride in being able to surround myself with incredible people in pursuit of a mutual goal. Every member of my team has skills that complement my own and make up for areas I'm lacking.

I'm a problem solver. I may not have all the answers, but if there's a problem, you can bet I'll find a solution!

Tell me about a weakness or personal character flaw, and what you're doing to overcome it?

In the past, I often trusted people too quickly. One of my most significant weaknesses was not having the discernment to recognize when someone was not trustworthy. In an early business venture, I made the mistake of taking a group of "friends" at their word. Unfortunately, my trust was poorly founded, and one of them preyed on my goodwill to illegally take control of my company. Although he did end up in prison for his crimes, I lost a multi-million dollar opportunity in the process. I still trust people, but I have learned to get every agreement in writing to protect myself in business.

How do you make important decisions?

I've never been an impulsive person. I try to pray for guidance and weigh risk versus benefit to make crucial decisions. I created a modified version of a pros and cons sheet for myself, like the method Benjamin Franklin used. My version also includes urgency, importance, and cost to calculate whether an opportunity is worth taking.

Was there a pivotal moment that set you on the path to where you are now?

As a teenager, my mom used to take my little brother and me to business seminars and conferences. We heard from speakers like Robert Kiyosaki, Zig Ziglar, John C. Maxwell, Dr. Robert Rohm, Gary Chapman, Les Brown, and others. From a very young age, these powerhouse mentors inspired me. I knew my path in life was that of an entrepreneur.

Are there any books you've read more than once? Why?

I've read the book, "How to Win Friends and Influence People" by Dale Carnegie more than a dozen times. I've also re-read "Rich Dad Poor Dad" by Robert Kiyosaki and "The Five Love Languages" by Gary Chapman several times. I often re-read books so I can remind myself of essential details.

Tell me about a difficult commitment you've made, and would you make it again?

I've sacrificed years of energy and financial resources to develop different companies, but the most challenging commitment was building Best Cellular. As the company grew and expanded nationwide, we borrowed hundreds of thousands of dollars while taking little (or no) pay.

We knew we were competing against billion-dollar corporations. We had nothing but sheer willpower and a shoe-string budget. Our CFO (Paul Silzell) and my parents all worked countless hours for no compensation while spending their retirement savings on growing the company. My parents lived in the back of the

16

Hotchkiss store while I lived in another one of the retail stores. I had no shower, no kitchen, slept on a futon mattress in the back storage room and showered at the gym for almost three years to save money so we could grow the company.

It was far more difficult than we imagined, but we've seen the lives of so many of our employees and customers affected positively. I would make the sacrifice again!

What character traits do you value most in others?

I am inspired by those who seek to possess traits of humility, modesty, diligence, and imagination. I admire those who take risks, and especially those who practice self-discipline. In the book of Proverbs, it says,

> "Get wisdom. Though it may cost all you have, get understanding."

I value courage, honesty, and integrity. I respect those who are willing to stand up and do what is right, even when it's unpopular. Loyalty and commitment mean a lot to me. I'm always inspired when I meet a couple who have been married for 40 years or someone who's been a critical player in the same company for their entire career.

How do you push through your worst times?

As anyone with diabetes will attest, glucose fluctuations cause mood swings.

The brain tumor I survived also caused severe depression, short-term memory loss, and loss of energy. I had to do something to stay upbeat. Positive books and podcasts have played a considerable role in keeping me motivated, even in the worst times.

What keeps you awake at night?

I think a lot about how to be a positive influence on the lives of my friends, family, employees, and those reading my books. I continuously study to improve and want to ensure that I leave a positive legacy for those I encounter.

In the early days, we spent a lot of sleepless nights, figuring out how to make payroll and cover expenses and take care of our excellent team. Any successful entrepreneur can relate to the early stages of their business. They could see the vision, and the company was growing like crazy, but there simply wasn't enough money to cover all the costs.

I had to learn how to be the kind of person that attracted incredible employees like the ones we have now, even though there wasn't enough money to pay them what they were worth.

What inspires you?

Hustlers and go-getters inspire me. I'm inspired not only by winners but more so by those who refuse to give up. I love supporting the "underdog." It inspires me to see someone take a risk that no one else understands, and watch them work their guts out to accomplish it, even if no one else believes in their cause (until they succeed). I get incredibly motivated listening to talks given by passionate people who are living their dreams.

How do you manage and prioritize opportunities?

People often approach me with ideas that "could make a lot of money." We have to recognize our strengths and our limitations.

I study trends in the economy and keep an eye on competitors who are succeeding and those who are experiencing failure to capitalize on cultural trends and demands. Even what political parties are in office can be a determining factor in whether a business will thrive or fail. I view every financial decision as a calculated risk and strive to weigh the risk versus benefit of each opportunity.

Recently, someone approached me looking for an investment in an organic fish hatchery. He said he could guarantee a 225% return on my investment. That may have been an incredible opportunity for the right investor. I don't know anything about fish, or the risks and expenses involved in operating fish hatcheries, so I declined. It may have been an incredible opportunity, but it wasn't a risk I would be comfortable investing in.

What advice would you give to your 18-year-old self?

Nothing is out of your reach. Failure isn't final. I love the saying,

"You learn more from failure than from

success. Don't let it stop you. Failure
builds character."

There were periods in my life when I'd
devoted too much time and energy to
projects that simply wouldn't succeed no
matter how hard I worked. Another piece of
advice I'd share is to know when to cut
your losses and move on.

CHAPTER 5

Don't Take Ownership Of Misfortune

Although an endocrinologist diagnosed me with Type 1 (insulin-dependent) diabetes at 27 months old, my mom had the foresight to make sure I didn't let it define me. She urged me not to say things like, "my diabetes is making me feel bad."

She gave me the same advice in 2011 when I was diagnosed with a malignant glioblastoma brain tumor. Saying things like, "my cancer," "my brain tumor," or "my cancer treatment" means you're taking ownership of the hardship and making it yours. Although dealing with brain cancer was a tough break, she reminded me that it shouldn't define me. My parents immediately began researching alternative treatment methods instead of settling for the misfortune of hearing that I only had a few months to live.

People often complain about depression or poor health. When you say things like, "my depression is terrible this year," it tells your subconscious that you are a depressed person. This statement affirms in your mind that depression is a part of who you are, and tells you that you will never rise above it. We all get tough breaks in life. But you don't have to take ownership of misfortune you didn't create!

Take Charge Of Your Life

Do not think or assume that what happens to you is your destiny. It is not! Don't let hardships or setbacks determine what you can accomplish. Stop saying things like, "I have bad luck." Quit thinking you have bad genetics or that you aren't smart enough to achieve great things. You are in charge of your life. You are responsible for your destiny. God made you awesome, and there are things that no one else can do as good as you can!

Science proves that people who have an optimistic outlook on life have a significantly reduced risk of dying from cancer, heart disease, stroke, respiratory disease, and infection. Better health is just one side effect of choosing to have a positive outlook on life. Taking charge of your life starts with your attitude.

Surround yourself with positive influences, and it will affect your outlook. Offer to buy lunch or coffee to chat with a successful friend or colleague. Ask them what steps they take daily, to stay motivated and accountable for their success. This is an easy way to expand your circle of influence and learn from people who have already taken charge of their own lives.

Life Is A Test

To be clear, I don't believe in the "prosperity gospel." God didn't promise that good things would happen just because you hope for them. You have to take decisive, consistent action to achieve your goals. In the Bible, God didn't say that life will be easy; in fact, He said quite the opposite:

"We must go through many hardships to

enter the kingdom of God." Acts 14:22

That's not to say that you can't win at life, just that you need to do the best with what you're given. In Matthew chapter 25, the "Parable of the Talents" tells of a master leaving his house to travel. Before he left, the master entrusted his property to three of his servants. When he returned, there were either rewards or consequences according to how they managed the talents each of them received. This story perfectly illustrates personal responsibility. We may not have received the same skills or the same amount of resources as someone else. However, we are each accountable for what we do with the time and abilities we are given.

Focus On Your Blessings

Self-help writer Edmond Mbiaka once said:

"It's impossible to notice how blessed you are if you are always focusing on your weaknesses and obstacles."

A negative mindset is very limiting. Just like a horse wearing blinders, your focus can only be in one direction at a time. If your goal is to succeed in life, aim for it! Focusing on your blessings and working past your "issues" allows you to move towards your goals. Stop concentrating on your shortcomings. Take stock and be grateful for the strengths and blessings you have already received.

Stop Comparing Yourself To Others

Social media has created a global community of people who live to compare themselves to each other. Unfortunately, this rampant narcissism can skew our perception of ourselves, in light of the false image other people are projecting. Dave Ramsey likes to say:

"We buy things we don't need with money we don't have to impress people we don't like."

Everyone has struggles and shortcomings. Don't let filtered pictures on social media or boastful, fake entrepreneurs driving rented luxury cars make you feel like you can't compare. The truth is: In real life, even they don't compare to their social media profiles. The "Photoshop culture" we see online is not reality. Measure your success by actual results. Don't compare yourself to a false reality promoted by people who haven't even achieved the lifestyle they're selling.

God put greatness inside of each of us. If you haven't found your calling yet, start searching for what you were meant to do - and do it better than anyone else!

CHAPTER 6

Interview with Jeff "Biggs" Wobig (US Navy SEAL sniper)

Jeff Wobig is a former US Navy SEAL sniper and member of the elite Navy SEAL Team 5, as well as Navy SEAL Team 7. Jeff is a skilled leader and an accomplished entrepreneur.

Jeff "Biggs" Wobig is also the co-founder and director of Global Accuracy/CTS Solutions. The company has offered tactical advising and security consulting to the United States Government on highly classified projects. Global Accuracy/CTS Solutions has expanded its services to the private sector due to the high demand from VIP clients.

Mr. Wobig was involved in the development of the Remington Custom Shop SIXSITE edition rifle. Jeff won the Maximum Warrior competition by Maxim Magazine and "Best of the Best" Special Ops, representing the US Navy and the SEAL community.

Jeff "Biggs" Wobig has been featured on TV shows such as "Battleground: Rhino Wars," which debuted on Animal Planet. Jeff, along with other Navy SEALs and a Green Beret, made a substantial impact during this project, taking down seven crime syndicates and imparting essential skills to their South African counterparts.

Below are some insights from Jeff "Biggs" Wobig. Enjoy!

What is your definition of success?

I am under the assumption that failure is impossible as long as you do not quit. My definition of success is constant progress. If you can do something to better yourself daily, then you are successful. As long as you can always persevere, as long as you can still continue to find some way to become more, that's it.

When did you consider yourself a success?

I believe that my success ebbs and flows. I can't live on yesterday. I have to live for today and the future. There have been times I may have been perceived as a success, but I was receding from a successful position. I would say that I've had the ability to be successful since I came into this world. I have dominated portions of my life, and I've stooped in a couple of areas, taking two steps back and one step forward at certain times.

Self-analyzing helps out: knowing where I'm at, knowing where I want to go, setting my goals, and achieving those goals. When I do that, or I'm working towards a goal, I feel as if I'm successful. But, I have to have a goal first. I have to have a mission. So, my challenges are always keeping myself goal-oriented and shooting for the stars.

What steps do you take daily to improve?

I'm afraid of routine. Routine kind of freaks me out a little bit. At the same time, I implement a little bit of routine just to make sure that I'm living a healthy and happy life. My steps to improve daily focus on my overall happiness and the happiness of those that I love. How I can make that happen dictates what I do daily to improve. My goal at this point in my life is the pursuit of happiness. I think that every individual has a different definition of happiness and success. That's just mine.

When I wake up, I like to thank God, say a prayer, and be grateful. I do a breathing exercise (where I re-oxygenate my brain), drink some water, and work out immediately within the first two minutes of getting out of bed. I like to do something that makes me sweat, and that's it. It doesn't have to be horrible.

The thing about my personality is that I'm kind of like a freight train. It takes me a lot to get started, but once I'm going, it takes a lot to get me to stop. So, if I can just get started in the morning, I have a great day. If I don't get started in the morning, then my whole day suffers because of it. Starting right is essential!

Building a good foundation in your life is essential. Build a good foundation every day. There are different foundations. You create a life foundation, a year foundation, a month foundation, and a day foundation. Then you can build an hour foundation. Work off of that to get through one minute of your life. It's not just getting through, but it's dominating every minute of your life that counts.

It's easy to get through, but it's essential to want to dominate because that's your goal. Then you ask yourself, "Do I dominate life?" I choose what domination of my life means. It's not a bad term. It means I'm willing to dominate my goal for that day. Other things that I do are to improve or just self-analyze. I'm honest with myself because I know when I'm not operating at 100 percent. Rarely ever am I actually rolling out at 100 percent, but if I can get up in the 90s or even the 80s, that's an awesome day.

Have a plan. The Teams say, "Plan your dive, dive your plan." That's kind of how I try to do it.

What have you recognized as your greatest strengths, and how have they impacted your success?

I have been blessed with physical strengths, but I don't rely on them as heavily as I do my mental strength. My most considerable strengths come from stubbornness and always wanting to be an outsider. I've always wanted to be on the outside. I've never wanted to be normal.

I never wanted to hang out with the flock. I've always been a sheepdog on the outside of the flock. That came to me naturally from a very young age. I didn't identify with all the people around me. I liked them, enjoyed them, and wanted to be friends with them, but I just knew we were different. At school, I knew that some of my teachers were living their dream, and some of them were miserable at their job. I saw that at an early age and realized that I don't want to be miserable in life, no matter what I do.

Foresight has been a considerable

strength of mine. I like to gain knowledge and retain wisdom.

The ability to manage stress is also a strength of mine. I said it before, and I'll say it again: I've never seen "freaking out" work out well for anybody. You're never going to be able to go back in time. If something happened, you're not gonna' be able to change it. So figure it out, but "freaking out" is not going to help anything. Remain cool, calm, and collected. Take care of business.

I'd say another strength of mine: I love ferociously. I love God fiercely, and I love my family and my friends. That's the motivation that gets you up when you don't want to get up. When you have nothing else to drive for, you drive for others. We can live with our own pain, but it's hard to live with other people's pain. I like to keep my family and friends out of pain. That's a motivator for me. I'll do anything I can to ensure that the people around me are living a good life, living a happy life, and feeling loved, because they are.

Tell me about a weakness or personal character flaw, and what you're doing to overcome it?

I could go on and on about weaknesses. I don't like to call them weaknesses as much as things that I would personally like to change. Some shortcomings could be other people's strengths. Some of my character flaws are considered a weakness. My weaknesses shouldn't be blanketed across everybody's character, because everybody's different.

I have an administrative weakness: I shouldn't be around paperwork. I don't do well with it since I'm full-fire and not a lot of water. But God did something for me early on. He paired me with a wife who has a lot in common with me, but we're the exact opposite in some areas. One of them is that she's administratively powerful. I'm driven. That completes our personality profile and puts us in a position where we can work together as entrepreneurs. It helps us to run businesses because I need a personality that enjoys paperwork or that can do it. I shut down if it seems mundane and boring. It looks like a waste of time to me. That's my weakness.

I work on trying to be the best me I can be. Life can get in the way of being in a good mood or making the best decisions. Those decisions being ones that make you happier and make the people around you happy. I've made plenty of choices that don't do either of those. That's a weakness. We should always try to bring positivity into the world and leave the negativity out. I've been working on that goal for a long time, but I still slip. I think we all do and always will. We're not perfect, but that's something I would like to overcome daily.

How do you make important decisions?

I am very analytical, so I like to crunch the numbers. I would consider that the strength of seeing the big picture, looking at the full spectrum of the problem, and finding a full-spectrum solution. Ultimately, the most significant work successes that I've had came from being a problem solver. That's probably my reputation at this point. I'm known as an effective problem solver. A lot of that comes from my time in the Teams, where there's never a problem you can't circumvent. "No" is not an answer. You never quit. There's always a solution. It takes a little bit of work, and you have to find it, but there is a solution.

Going back to the original question, it depends on what that important decision entails. If it's a financial decision, then it's about the numbers. It's about whether the juice is worth the squeeze. It's that simple. If it's a personal decision, then it's a lot harder. It involves the heart and emotions, and they are a lot harder to deal with than numbers and laws.

Was there a pivotal moment that set you on the path to where you are now?

If there was one pivotal moment that set me on the path to where I am now, it was becoming a US Navy SEAL. It was completing the training and putting in the work upfront. I say that to people in business all the time. When you put the work in upfront, it will pay dividends on the backside. That's what I have personally seen in everything I've done.

It could be a job: You go to college first, getting your degree, and understand the trade that you're going into, or the military sets you on that path. It could be raising children right, where you're putting in all the hard work upfront so that they become good adults. That's what BUD/S was for me, a lot of hard work upfront. It set me on a path where I could know who I was and what I was capable of because I put myself through the test. It's not that I didn't know before, but I confirmed it. Sometimes we need that self-affirmation.

If you wanted to pinpoint one moment in my professional career, I would say it was this: I was raised in an extremely loving home that did not put an emphasis on money. The perception of our community may have been that we were in poverty. The worldly view may have seen us as impoverished, but I know that I was loved. That worldly view can hang with you. When you go to a public school in a small town, there's a division of the "have's" and "have-not's." We were in the latter group, and I didn't appreciate people trying to tell me my capabilities because of my parents' desired lifestyle.

I decided when I was very young that nobody could tell me what to do or what not to do in this life. I knew I was a good person. I knew I had a good soul. Then I knew that nobody could tell me what I can and can't do. Plenty of them tried, and I still can hear their voices in my head when they say, "You're gonna' be nothing. You're going to go to prison when you grow up."

I was at a funeral in my Navy blues, with my Trident and my awards on, which is rare for us to wear. Those are usually only for a funeral, but it was for a local man that was in the Navy and passed away. A very close family friend and an elderly woman came up to me and started shaking my hand. Then everybody was excited to shake my hand and thank me for my service, which I appreciated. A woman came up and said, "You know, I'm very proud of you. I thought you were going to prison." That made me pretty mad. It's one of the rudest things anybody has ever said to me. I didn't want to talk to her anymore.

She said, "Do you know who I am?" I said, "No, I don't." She said, "I knew you when you were in elementary school." She wasn't a great person. She wasn't a great person because I remember her trying to steal my dreams. I know that as an adult now. She came back and tried to buddy-up with me, and I didn't appreciate it. Yet she was one of the driving factors for why I wanted to succeed. I guess I can thank her for that.

That's one of those things I tell my children. There are dream thieves everywhere, but nobody can steal your dreams if you don't let them. As far as pivotal moments go that set me on my path, there were plenty of them. I would say that a lot of it came from the negativity I received from our social status as a child. I didn't want to be stuck there for life. I knew my family was good people. Some of the kids that were given preferential treatment didn't have good parents. They weren't overachievers. They were getting something for nothing.

Sometimes people say, "Fake it till you make it." I'm okay with that. To a certain extent, you can fake it till you make it. But at some point, you're just a fake. Make sure you make it at some point. I never want to be a fake. I've always wanted to be authentic, genuine, and real. Those are some goals I have.

We homeschool our children. My wife talks about how if you send your kids to school, their peers tell them what they're going to be in life. It's true. If you're a witty little kid or an outspoken extrovert versus an introverted kid, then you get to tell the introverts what they're going to be. That's not right. They're talented and gifted in different ways. In a setting like that, the squeaky wheel gets the grease, and that's not how it should be. I like the quote from Abraham Lincoln,

"It's better to remain silent and be thought a fool than to speak and to remove all doubt."

You know what, that just doesn't apply to elementary school children or grade school. At a young age, I was able to identify that "Hey, this is backward, and I don't have to listen to this." I realized that I could be whoever I want to be, and nobody can tell me otherwise.

Moving through high school, everybody just gets to tell you what they're going to be. Then they get to identify as that profession. They say, "I'm going to be a professional basketball player" even though you and I know they were average (at best) at a small school in Colorado. You'd say, "Well, that's probably not going to happen..." I still think that's a slim chance, right? We're gonna' call it really really slim. Maybe it's about the same odds as the "goo, to the zoo, to you theory" (theory of evolution), you know?

Anyway, not to diverge. I guess I was getting at this point: Even in high school, kids were saying, "I'm going to do this, and I'm going to do that," but I was still realistic. I didn't want to steal something that I hadn't earned yet. I didn't say I was gonna' be a NAVY Seal. I said, "I'm going to go to SEAL training. I would like to be a Navy SEAL. That's my dream. That's my goal. I want to be a Navy SEAL." It hadn't been determined yet, right? And it just helps you to work hard for that goal.

Don't claim your trophy before you earn it, or else you'll stop working for it. It's perceived success, and you almost believe your lie. At some point, that's dangerous. If you start believing your own lie, you'll stop working towards the truth. You'll be miserable in that as well. Work has almost become a bad word in our society. Work is healthy. It's what we're supposed to do. I like to think of the Seven Dwarfs and how they're just happy. They're delighted to whistle as they go to work every day. That's what we should all be doing.

Find something you love to do, and do it. If you don't love to work, it's because you haven't given it a shot. Change your habits! For three weeks straight, get up early, work your butt off all day and see if your life improves. See if you're happier. If you're not pursuing happiness, then what the heck are you doing? If you want to be miserable, be miserable somewhere else because I don't want to hear your negativity anyway.

Are there any books you've read more than once? Why?

Yeah, there are a couple of books I've read more than once. Most of them are instructional. I'll read books on shooting. I'm a long-range shooting instructor and have a passion for long-range shooting. I'm debatably okay at it. [Editor's Note: We mentioned earlier that

Jeff won the Maximum Warrior competition by Maxim Magazine and "Best of the Best" Special Ops, representing the US Navy and the SEAL community.]

There are different stages in life that I've gone through. I went through a phase of preparation, so I read a particular book two or three times while overseas. It was a really neat story about prepping and fighting for the Union. That was interesting to me at the time, probably ten years ago.

There are some financial books that I've read a couple of times. I've read Rich Dad Poor Dad a few times; I thought that was an excellent book. Robert Kiyosaki wrote that. I've read some inspirational books. I've also read some Team guys' books, which I try not to read very much. A couple of my friends have written books on their experiences in the Teams, and I'll read through them a couple of times to be sure I'm giving them solid feedback on their material.

Tell me about a difficult commitment you've made, and would you make it again?

Three main commitments that I've made were my commitment to God, my commitment to my wife, and my commitment to the US while serving in the US Navy. As far as the most significant commitments, I wouldn't change any of them. They've all put a lot of value in my life.

What character traits do you value most in others?

I think loyalty is the most important trait and the first to be overlooked. Nobody appreciates loyalty as they should. That's the first thing to be forgotten. It's tough since the people that are most loyal to you are often the easiest to hurt. You know there are limited repercussions, or you assume that there are limited repercussions because that person has been so loyal and so kind to you. It's an easier solution sometimes for CEOs to dump the loyal guy for the bottom line. I think that's a mistake. You can't replace loyalty, and you can't buy loyalty. That's important.

I think integrity is also essential. Honesty, humility, all of those are fundamental to me. A balance of good traits is important, as well. You can't just be a good person or a good friend. You can't just be super loyal. You can't just be super honest. You need to have a couple of good traits behind you if you want to be a good person.

Lastly, I would say morality. I want somebody who's moral. That's important because if you can't hold to your moral compass, how will I ever trust you? Trust is important.

How do you push through your worst times?

Never give up, man! Quitting is never an option, ever. You have to put that in your mind! I can relate to not quitting, going through BUD/S where the attrition rate is 80%. It's very tough. If you tell yourself quitting is an option, you're going to quit. If you give yourself an out, you're gonna' take the out. The simple solution to that is never to give yourself an out. If you want to get something done, say, "I will get that done, and I will not stop until it's done." Just embrace the suck and go for it.

You know that there's going to be brighter skies. The worst-case scenario is, you die, and that can't be the worst-case scenario because if you're a firm believer in Jesus Christ, you're going to a better place. So stop worrying, be happy. How do I push through the worst times? Of course, I have bad times, but I guess I also rely on my past experiences. I've been through some tough times. I believe everybody has.

Life is hard for everybody. So if you can look back at something, either voluntary or involuntary, that was tough on you; maybe you thought, "Man, the world is ending. It's over. I just want to die. I just don't want to be here anymore. This is horrible. I don't want to be in this situation." Whatever that horrible, rock-bottom feeling you had was, you know that it was temporary and you got through it. I look back at those moments and say, "Man, that was miserable."

If a friend dies or gets killed, it's powerfully emotional. I can only imagine being divorced or losing loved ones. Whatever the worst-case scenario is, if you can think about that or think about how you got through a very negative situation, odds are you'll get through this one. That's part of dealing with stress, knowing you only have control over so many things. The only time you hit your knees is to pray. Even if you get knocked to your knees, get right back up.

It's just one step at a time and one

second at a time. When I was going through BUD/S, there were times when one more day was too much. One more hour? Sometimes one more hour's too much. One more minute? Sometimes every second was miserable. But in the time it took me to say "one more second," I was already three seconds in. I only had to say that 20 times to get me to a minute.

Usually, within a couple of minutes, we were back up out of the water on our feet and running again. Our minds were changing. You can break it down incrementally, to the smallest step possible. You can take it one second at a time until you build up enough tenacity to push yourself to a minute. Push yourself to 5 minutes, 10 minutes, an hour, a day, a week, a month, a year, a decade, a life.

What keeps you awake at night?

I don't stress, but I don't sleep well. That's an issue that I'm working to fix. I don't have PTSD. I don't have any issues with the things I've done in war. I just have trouble shutting my mind off. So I would say what keeps me awake at night would only be a busy mind and continuously wanting to solve problems. I'm a problem solver, so I'm always searching for those solutions. I believe that going to sleep with a thoughtful mind helps you to wake up with solutions. You know, in your subconscious, you're working at finding the solution to that problem.

Your brain is a fantastic tool. We were created amazingly. Let that thing work for you. The problem is, sometimes I try to overload it before I go to sleep. I'm so excited to get up and find a solution or continue working. I would say that it's not cool not to sleep. I'm taking measures to sleep as much as possible. It's a health concern at this point, not sleeping enough. It's not right; that's not good. So I would say that sleep habits are what keep me up at night. I just need better sleep, and that's something that we can control. That's a problem I can solve.

What inspires you?

Oh man, inspiring people inspire me. God inspires me. The world inspires me. Nature inspires me. The high that you get from doing good in this world inspires me. I love seeing the joy on other people, whether it be men, women, or children; it's just beautiful to see joy. That inspires me. That's what drives me to make money, the ability to gift, and whatever those gifts are, which aren't always financial gifts. I'm not saying you have to have money to give gifts. I'm saying that's the different levels of gifting that I can apply, whether it's buying a piece of land where my kids can go out and play, or buying a bicycle for a kid to play on, or tithing, or whatever. That's what inspires me. As far as finances go, it's happiness. Happiness inspires me.

I always say two things drive: desperation or inspiration. I would rather be inspired than desperate. Look at what you want. Look at what you need. Understand the difference. Once you have what you need, strive to succeed continually. Continually progress until you have what you want. As long as you have what you need (the basics of food, water, and shelter), you can focus on what inspires you.

I'm a blessed person. So I look at my giftings, and I don't want to take them for granted. I don't want to abuse this wonderful place that we live in and not enjoy what was created for us to enjoy and have a wonderful time. Knowing that I was put here by a loving God that wants me to have fun and wants me to enjoy myself and be happy inspires me. If I'm not happy, I'm letting Him down, and that's letting me down and letting my family down. That's disappointing, and I don't want to be a disappointment.

How do you manage and prioritize opportunities?

I will take on the opportunity that I am best prepared for first. I need to analyze how fast I can become prepared for that opportunity. That's a secret of success: you don't wait for an opportunity to prepare yourself for it. You prepare yourself for the opportunity, so when it presents itself, you're ready to go. Know your gifts and your strengths and your weaknesses. Know if it's something that fits your abilities, or if it's something you're forcing yourself into for financial gain or pride.

I manage my priorities by what I'm capable of doing, my desire to get it done, and the preparation I put in on the front side.

I'm not saying if an opportunity arises that you can't prepare for it or not do it, I'm saying be ready for it. If you wanted to be an actor, you don't just walk around the streets of Hollywood until some producer or some casting agent says, "Hey,

I think you'd be great in a movie!" If that happens, and you truly wanted to be an actor, I would hope you had gone to some acting school before that, and you're ready to be an actor.

If you want to be a Navy SEAL, don't show up fat and out of shape friggin' saying, "Oh, I'll run tomorrow." You need to be running a couple of years out in front of that, getting ready, preparing yourself. When the Navy calls up and says, "Hey, you're in. Let's go. You've got BUD/S class coming up in six months." Well, you better be ready. You don't friggin' wait till the last minute to prepare yourself.

So how do I manage and prioritize opportunities? If it's financial, I crunch the numbers. Is the juice worth the squeeze? What is the end-state of that opportunity? Is it a true opportunity? Is it a blessing, or is it a curse in disguise? Sometimes the best opportunities, or what appears to be the best opportunities, can be the most damaging thing that you can put your business through. My personal quote is,

"You only know what you've experienced, everything else you've been taught."

I only know what I've experienced. A lot of my decision making comes from the experiences that I've had, and personal experiences that I know to be a fact in this life. I know people more than I know opportunities. If I sense something is wrong with the sell or the spiel, if it looks too good to be true, usually it is. There's a lot of truth to that. So I'm able to look at something full-spectrum and know if it's good for my business, family, friends, or goals.

People say, "If someone needs your help, you help them." I agree to a certain extent. I'm not trying to sound like a hardened soul, but this is important for anybody who's growing in business and growing in finance, especially when you've come from nothing. You understand the pain that can come from not having any kind of financial support, right? The worst thing you can do when you're first starting to bring in revenue is to be what I would call a "financial martyr."

A "financial martyr" is a guy who makes his first 100 grand and buys his mom a $50,000 car. Is he a wonderful person? One hundred percent. Does he have a good heart? One hundred percent! He's got a great heart, and he's a good friend. You probably want to be friends with that guy. He sounds like a great guy, but is he gonna' continue to help people? Probably not, because he's gonna' be broke. There's also a fine line between not being a "financial martyr" and being greedy. There's a difference. Don't cripple yourself to heal another.

As a protector and as a father, I can tell you that I'll fight the fight. Don't worry; I'm there. I'll fight the fight, but I've got to be able to fight. I've got to be able to stay in the fight. So I have to keep myself healthy. I don't know if I'd call it a secret, but it doesn't seem to be common knowledge. A lot of good people don't ever bankroll anything because they try to save one life instead of 1,000. I'm not saying that if your kid needs a hospital bill paid, you don't do whatever it takes. Sometimes that one life is the most important thing to you. It's not always a numbers game.

Right now, if my financial knees got knocked out from under me, I'm okay. I have a loving wife and loving children. We'll live out in the middle of the forest, and I'll start over from nothing. It's really cool to find out how to make money because nobody can take that away from you. You can take all my money from me, but you cannot take away my ability to make more. Once you find the "secret sauce," you can always use it again. That's freedom, right?

I feel like I'm kind of going off on tangents. The simple answer to the question of how do you manage and prioritize your opportunities is this: Analyze the opportunity. What's the most bang for the buck? What has the most substantial return for the smallest investment? There are so many variables. We could be here all day talking about them, but that's just something that you have to learn from personal experience or a mentor's experiences to help you make that decision.

What advice would you give to your 18-year-old self?

To be honest with you, if I could tell my 18-year-old self (or any 18-year-old) how to live life, that would be, "Live life to the fullest. Enjoy every day because it's fun! Be a good person." That would be an extremely important thing. Just be a good person. Everybody knows what a good person is. Just do that. Be kind, but not weak. Be loving, be strong.

As far as business goes, I would say the

same thing: "Put in the hard work upfront. Work hard. Enjoy working." On a more serious note, I would say that it's not all about business. It's not all about money. Life is better than that, and it can end in a split second. So I would say that you should always let the people that mean the most to you, know how much they mean to you, and how much you love them. Let them know you care about them and that you appreciate them.

Going back to talk to the 18-year-old me and knowing what I was going to go through in my 20's as a Navy SEAL fighting in the war on terror, I would say, "Hang on. It's a wild ride." I think life's a wild ride, but it's enjoyable.

I would say, "There is a Creator, 100% guaranteed - and He loves you!" I would tell the younger me to rely on prayer more. I think that would help me out a lot with some of the difficulties I had.

While I was in the Navy, I didn't have a care in the world about money. I didn't figure I would ever live to see 30, so why save money? You know, it might have helped me out financially a bit, but maybe it kept me hungry. That goes back into that "don't be a financial martyr." I can speak to that on some level of experience because I didn't mind draining my account every two weeks. I got paid every 14 days, and every 15th day I was broke. So I didn't have the best financial literacy at the time, but I had a good time. I don't know that I would change any of that.

"Give open-heartedly." That was something I had to learn later. Being in the Navy, I didn't have a lot to give as far as money went. I have always been a gifter. I always liked to give gifts. Some people are like that, and some people aren't. It's just something I do. I love to give. It makes me feel good. I would probably tell my 18-year-old self just to give it all away.

CHAPTER 7

Practice Delayed Gratification

Practicing delayed gratification means resisting the temptation of immediate rewards. In exchange, you increase the possibility of a greater reward in the future. Most people are terrible at practicing delayed gratification. We live in a society that allows us to have what we want when we want it, even if we don't deserve it. For many of us, self-discipline, restraint, and self-control are difficult skills to attain.

For evidence, look at how many Americans are overweight. Currently, over 70% of Americans qualify as overweight or obese. Or, take a look at debt from financing new vehicles, smartphones, clothing, and vacations. 80% of Americans are in debt. Consumer Reports says that in 2013, 84.5% of all cars on the road were financed. Studies show that the practice of delayed gratification and success go hand in hand. People who can manage their immediate desires in their jobs, relationships, health, and finances typically thrive.

What Is Delayed Gratification?

For many people, the ability to wait for satisfaction isn't natural. Practicing delayed gratification involves a feeling of dissatisfaction. To those who haven't learned to control their impulses, it seems impossible. Choosing to have your reward now might feel nice, but managing your desires can result in bigger and better rewards. Delaying gratification improves self-control and helps you achieve long-term goals faster.

You may be familiar with the Stanford University marshmallow experiment. In this study, researchers placed children in a room with a marshmallow. The children were given an easy instruction: "You can eat the marshmallow now, or you can wait 15 minutes and receive two marshmallows." Children who could wait for the second marshmallow, without eating the first one, scored higher on standardized tests. They also had better health and were less likely to have behavior problems later in life.

Consider your behavior in light of this study. Can you wait for what you want? Or, do you determine your course of action based on what feels good right now? Can you stick with a project until completion, or do you give up halfway through? Think back to when you practiced delayed gratification, whether it was big or small. How did you feel afterward? Your patience reveals a lot about your character.

How To Practice Delayed Gratification

So how do you develop this skill? It can be as easy as finding something else more interesting than what is right in front of you. Through their "marshmallow research," the researchers noted a consistency within the group of kids who gave in. Their focus was entirely on the short-term. If they smelled the marshmallow, played with it, or pretended to eat it, they quickly caved to their desires and gobbled it up. But, those children who were able to shift their attention elsewhere succeeded. The kids found all sorts of imaginative ways to take their minds off the first marshmallow, even reminding themselves out loud of the reward for waiting.

Daydreaming is another tactic for practicing delayed gratification that might seem a bit counter-intuitive. If you occasionally let your mind wander, you will find it easier to connect with your long-term goals. Once you complete a project, take a mental break before diving into the next one. Take a walk to clear your head and revitalize your senses. Your future self will thank you.

What Are The Benefits of Practicing Delayed Gratification?

These small shifts in your thinking can lead to extraordinary changes in your life. Temptations will often pop up right in front of you unannounced. If you can distract yourself or find a dream to focus on, you will discover resisting those desires a lot easier. The key is to repeat these reactions until they become second nature. Then you can congratulate yourself for developing the habit of delaying gratification! The Bible recommends patience over military strength:

"Better a patient person than a warrior, one with self-control than one who takes a city." - Proverbs 16:32 NIV

49

Although the Stanford marshmallow study was initially run in the 1960s, practicing delayed gratification isn't a new idea. Aristotle, the eminent Greek philosopher, discovered in 300 BC that many people felt unhappy simply because they confused temporary comfort for lasting joy. He taught that true happiness stems from developing habits and relationships that enrich your life. According to Aristotle, this will allow you to progress towards your highest potential. Practice delayed gratification, rather than trying to feel good now. You will build a life of purpose.

CHAPTER 8

Reward Yourself

Many Americans live lavishly but finance their lifestyles with credit cards or high-interest rate loans. In this chapter, I'd like to connect with those of you on the other end of the spectrum, who deprive yourself to the point of making life almost unbearable. If you ignore the need to reward yourself, you will regret it later on!

I'm writing this from personal experience. I've always been working harder than necessary but never feeling like it was enough to deserve a reward. At times I made more money in one day than many of my friends had made in months. But even with that high income, I still lived in the back of one of my phone stores and drove a beat-up old truck. I refused to spend money on anything that wasn't building the business. I reasoned that since every dollar I put in generated a $3 return, I couldn't afford to spend money on myself! I've intentionally made changes to start enjoying life. In the last few years, I realized that "you can't take it with you." I realized it was okay to reward myself for a job well done.

Celebrate Your Achievements

Celebrating a milestone of success can help you move on to bigger and better things. If you always feel like your journey to success is a "hamster wheel," you can get burned out! Specific recognition for your accomplishments will provide "chapters" for your life story. Then you can take a break, breathe, and start on the next big thing. Remember that you can reward yourself many times along the way!

Get your friends involved. Whether it's a post on social media or a celebration at your place, your friends and loved ones want to celebrate with you! A time or event set aside can help you process the achievement. It also gives others a specific opportunity to express their gratitude for your hard work and dedication.

Reflect on what it took to reach your goal. Remember that success is a journey over time, but you will need to stop and rest to consider where you've come from. Some of the top entrepreneurs find it difficult to acknowledge their success. They focus so much on what's ahead that they never stop to enjoy where they are. Give yourself credit when you hit your goals!

Celebrate Your Team's Accomplishments

As a leader, praising your team or employees is just as important as rewarding yourself. Of course, you never want to ignore them while enjoying yourself! One of the most important things to remember is to make praise public. Vince Lombardi, the famous football coach, was known for saying:

"Praise in public, criticize in private."

Share specifics from the success stories of your team. This public praise will encourage them to push their limits. You can also highlight what works and even what doesn't within your strategy. The whole team can learn from the success of others. Make it detailed and include any relevant context. Consider adding a gift or reward for recognition. Something as simple as a pat on the back or a high-five can significantly impact your team's morale!

Reward Yourself Immediately

Being rewarded solidifies in your mind that your effort is worth the reward. Reward yourself and your team as soon as you complete a crucial task or reach a goal. Why is it so important to enjoy rewards as quickly as possible? This creates a definite link within your mind between the achievement and the reward. Every time you are facing similar stress or challenges in the future, your subconscious will remember the positive results. In this manner, you can create a habit of success! Even small rewards can be great motivators, whether that's a break for coffee, a short walk, or an evening out to dinner.

Choose Something You Enjoy

For many, personal rewards can lead to losing the ground they gained from their goals. Make sure your rewards aren't

counter-productive! Brainstorm for
potential recompenses that aren't just
money, but experiences as well. Take a bit
of time to figure out some prizes, and
make sure to take the chance to reward
yourself so you can enjoy the benefits of
your success!

CHAPTER 9

Interview with Connie Wyatt (CMO of Best Cellular)

Connie Wyatt is one of the most motivated, dedicated, and loyal people I've ever met. She serves as the Chief Marketing Officer of Best Cellular. I'm blessed that Connie Wyatt is my mom! I mentioned earlier in the book that I owe much of my success to her.

When I was a kid, we had almost nothing. Yet, she helped my little brother and me pick out a nice suit and tie from the local thrift store as she worked hard to save up money to take us to business seminars and leadership conferences. She bought leadership books, success books, and personal development books to teach us. While many kids got an allowance, my mom would instead put a few bucks in the back of a book for us. Reading a book was our way of earning money for things we wanted. Connie Wyatt became hugely successful in her own life, and I have her to thank for my desire to succeed.

Connie has trained horses to compete at high school, collegiate, and National Finals Rodeo contests. As a skilled communications expert, Connie helped grow Best Cellular from a single hometown store to a nationwide MVNO. She was recognized on satellite TV as "Salesman of the Quarter" for a national builder. Connie Wyatt is an expert in utilizing innovative marketing strategies to draw traffic and sales.

In her own words, "When Curtis asked me

to write a chapter for his book, I was very hesitant. I told him, 'People don't want to hear from me, they want to read about how very successful people did what they did.' Then I realized that we all have a story to tell. Each of us can teach others how we overcame adversity and rose above it. I hope someone will relate to my experiences and appreciate their journey."

Below are some insights from Connie Wyatt. Enjoy!

What is your definition of success?

My definition of success is working towards "Point B." Layout a timeline to reach your goal. Start at the target destination and work backward to today, where you're at Point A.

We have done as we envisioned Best Cellular and laid out our projections, goals, and timelines. We continue to do check-ups to see if we're hitting our goals and to make sure we don't head off on any rabbit trails! You have to "put your dreams in concrete and draw your goals in the sand." Chase the dream. It doesn't change, but you may have to move your goal lines a bit along the way to adjust for shifting circumstances.

Practice self-discipline to stay the course. Remind yourself that the shortest distance between two points is a straight line. If you can keep your Point B in mind, it's easier not to get off course! For me, "Point B" is Heaven. While I'm here, though, I focus more on what I have than what I don't have! It's more about what I put into life than what I get out of it.

When did you consider yourself a success?

Earthly success is a moving, evolving thing. Some days you feel extraordinary, only to have other times that you feel like a total failure. There are "mountaintop experiences" in business and relationships, financially and spiritually, but there are deep dark "valley moments" as well. When you are up on top of the mountain, looking out over the valleys, everything is magnificent!

Then you hit times of being down. Business is struggling, and the family is fighting, health is compromised, finances are horrible. But did you ever stop to think that it's while you're in the valley that you realize you can't do this alone? It's dark and cold down there, so you begin to search for help. You are now scared and thirsty. So much so that you cry out to God for help because it's been a long hard trip. But at the bottom of the mountain, at the lowest point, that's where you find water. Living water to replenish you and revive you, so you can begin the climb back up to the mountaintop.

To answer your question about when I considered myself a success, I'll probably be my own worst critic here on earth until I'm finally at my forever heavenly home!

What steps do you take daily to improve?

- I strive to read the Bible daily. It

keeps me grounded in truth, and after all, it is indeed the Book of Life.

- I study and research to stay up on industry trends.
- I try to get physical exercise daily. It clears my mind and improves my mood.
- I pray for God to direct my steps, my words, and even my thoughts toward the direction of His plan for my life and glorify Him in the things I do that day.

I once read about a man whose father, a well respected and trusted man, operated a grain mill for decades. All of the local farmers brought in their crops to sell at his mill. He would weigh the grain on the old scale he had used for years. The old man died, and his son took over the business. He painted the buildings, did some repairs, and also had the scale recalibrated. He learned that the old scale was off. The son realized his father had been shorting the farmers on their grain weights for years!

So the questions the author asked was:

1. Was the father dishonest all these years? Answer: No, because he didn't know the scales were off and therefore hadn't intentionally tried to steal from the farmers.
2. Would it be dishonest for the son to continue using the scale at the same (incorrect) weights that his father had used for years? Answer: Yes, because he now had new information to know that the scales were off. With that new knowledge came

accountability to correct the scales!

That's how I try to grow in my thinking and opinions and attitudes continually. When I learn that what I used to think was wrong, then I immediately correct my thinking. If necessary, I also apologize to anyone else whom I misled with incorrect information.

What have you recognized as your greatest strengths, and how have they impacted your success?

One of my greatest strengths is being able to pick myself up one more time than I get knocked down. If I can do that, I will always win!

I'm competitive, like my dad. Man, that side of the family competes on everything from who gets to the coffee shop first every morning, to who drinks the most cups, to who can "spin the biggest yarn" and get you to believe it! Growing up was a lot of fun because of the competition. Rodeoing, having a foot race at the rodeo, bucking bales out in the hayfield, playing volleyball at church camp, water skiing at the lake, or playing cards during the winter evenings, we were always trying to win.

Life is a competition. You compete for a good job to provide for your family's needs. You contend with mother nature's bugs, drought, and bad weather to try to grow a garden for food. You compete with pollution and chemicals and GMOs and preservatives to try to keep your body healthy, despite the food you eat. You compete with the other guys to win the

59

girl you want to marry, and then you compete with the kids for your wife's time and affection.

In high school, I set school records for the 50 and 100-yard dashes and competed at State on relay teams who also set school records. My family didn't come to watch me compete unless it was a rodeo, and I always knew that this could be my last meet, so I gave it everything I had. I still feel they made me do even more chores to try to get me to give up the sports, but that was also okay. I learned that there's a price to be paid for doing something you want to do, and it's worth it!

Years later, my little sister and brother-in-law were up at a church camp playing a volleyball game. I dove to save a spiked ball and skinned my knee, and another time dove and kept a ball from hitting the ground and skinned my elbow. I was having a blast. All of a sudden, my sister remarked, "Connie, why do you always do that?"

I was confused and asked, "Do what?" She said, "Everyone is out here having fun playing ball, but you play like your life depends on it like it's the last game you're ever going to play! Why do you play so hard?" I thought about my answer for about two seconds and replied, "Because it just might be." I believe you should be "in it to win it" in everything you do!

Another strength of mine is being able to make most projects fun. I figure if you have to get the job done, you might as well enjoy the journey! You could be irritable and cranky and make it a miserable experience for yourself and everyone around you. You can also turn it into an opportunity to create comradery and appreciation for helping others get their part done. You'll create a team atmosphere. Most importantly, you can model love for each other. You'll find things to laugh about together as you muck through, completing the job, and then express genuine appreciation for their part in it!

The last thing I would say is tenacity. Many times in my life, I was called hardheaded, stubborn, or told that I didn't know when to stop hitting the wall and give it up. Many years later, I met some very successful business leaders who would say that I had tenacity. (I have to admit that I had to look the word up because I'd never heard it before that moment!) These successful business owners would say that I was determined, persistent, and wouldn't give up when I hit a wall. Instead, I'd find a way to climb over, go around it, or dig a tunnel under that wall and do whatever it took to get to the other side! My God-given gift of never giving up meant I didn't need to apologize or feel defective!

Tell me about a weakness or personal character flaw, and what you're doing to overcome it?

You would probably get several paragraphs on this question by asking my husband or those who spend time around me! I saw a cartoon one time that showed a person standing in front of a bookshelf in a bookstore. There was one section that said, "How to Fix Yourself," and another called "How to Fix Your Spouse." The self-help section was still full of books, but "How to Fix Your Spouse" sold out! That's sort of human, to see others' flaws much more quickly than recognizing our own.

I've been described as being loyal to a fault by a close family member. I don't agree with that opinion, and I suspect the comment stemmed from a bit of jealousy. Nevertheless, I don't believe loyalty is a problem as long as the person you are loyal to is in tune with Biblical principles. If they've proven to be an honest, upright person of integrity, who hasn't betrayed my trust, then I'm loyal to them, and I've got their back through whatever happens. I need to be better at making those who feel like I'm loyal to a fault feel more included and loved.

I once read a summary that said, "The greatest evidence of genuine friendship is loyalty" (loving at all times). First Corinthians chapter 13 explains what true love is. Verse 7 says that love always protects, always trusts, always hopes, and always perseveres. Loyalty is part of loving. Give me a loyal friend over ten fair-weather friends any day.

I could name a lot of personal flaws. The one I'm working on the most now is the mistake of confiding whatever is irritating me about one person to another. It's not a positive solution to the problem. It causes the person I told to feel either stressed for me or question their feelings about the other person. It also must make them wonder if I'll share these details about that person to them, then what am I sharing about them with someone else? I am working on keeping my mouth shut when I'm feeling upset about someone else. I should be taking the problem to my Heavenly Father.

How do you make important decisions?

First, I pray. I pray for God to lead me in the direction I need to take, to help me make the decision that will benefit everyone involved. I ask for His guidance along each path I need to choose. Then I seek counsel and get advice from others who are discerning and wise. Then we pray together. If time allows, I sleep on it. It's amazing what a clear perspective I'll have after thinking it through and then giving myself a night for my brain to process the pros and cons.

I research and read up on the topic at hand, and try to glean any tidbits of information that make me re-think it. I pray up to it (the point at which I "pull the trigger"), and then I pray through it (the whole process that evolves after the decision). At work with Best Cellular, we often get on speakerphone and pray about our company's decisions, for the health and blessings of our customers, and each other and our families.

When I married my husband, Steve, he was a "package deal" with kids and grandkids included! One of my bonus daughters, Jessie, is an extremely wise, spirit-led lady who I can spend hours talking to. She is the most well-read person I know and has at least four books she's reading at any given time. She's involved in church Bible studies, and she reads her Bible daily.

She is brilliant and just fascinating to talk with. I was sharing a situation that had happened in our family with her. I asked her how I might have responded better or differently to the problem, trying to determine what to do. Jessie said one of the wisest things I've ever heard, and it was a tipping point in my decision making from then on. She said, "If you make your decisions backed by biblical principles, you can't be wrong."

I was at a business seminar once, and the speaker answered an atheist who asked, "Do you have to be a Christian to be successful in business?" He said, "You don't have to believe in Jesus Christ to own or operate a business. But, to be hugely successful in any business, you must do what Jesus taught!" You have to do unto others as you would want them to do to you. You have to love other people, be kind, be honest, be compassionate, and be fair.

Was there a pivotal moment that set you on the path to where you are now?

Yes. My oldest son, Curtis, was diagnosed with brain cancer. That was in addition to living with Type 1 Juvenile Diabetes. He also had grand mal seizures daily. He lived alone and came close to death more times than I care to remember. At the time of his diagnosis, the neurologists gave us zero hope of survival. They advised us just to try to make him comfortable.

We had to make some tough decisions. We had to convince Curtis to walk away from his life in Denver and move in with us in a 100-year-old one-room log cabin, 35 miles from the nearest stoplight. He slept on the living room floor on a plastic mattress that would go flat every night. There was no phone service, no social contact, and with the brain issues, he couldn't even remember how to drive to the closest convenience store 7 miles from the cabin. Talk about a low point in his life!

I made him a promise: If he survived cancer, we would help him figure out a business he could do despite his health issues, and we would help him. We researched until we decided on the Hoxsey Biomedical Center in Tijuana, Mexico, for treatment because we had nothing to lose. Very long story condensed: that was eight years ago, and he survived and is cancer-free! He has residual scar tissue, so there are some lingering problems, but we continue to learn workarounds.

When it looked like we were winning the cancer battle, Curtis said, "I think I should open a cellular store." So we kept our word and helped. Little did we know that it would grow from a tiny little hometown store, with him living in the back of that first one, to become an MVNO (Mobile Virtual Network Operator). Best Cellular is now a nationwide business that's growing as fast as we can keep up! That decision has undoubtedly changed the course of mine and my husband's lives. It's hard work and long hours, but we know how truly blessed we are, and what a blessing the Best Cellular stores have been to us, to the customers, and the staff.

Are there any books you've read more than once? Why?

Yes, one of them is The Five Love Languages by Dr. Gary Chapman. That book helped me recognize how other people were showing me love, in their way that I previously hadn't realized. I was waiting for them to love me the way I would have shown love to them! Conversely, I was working hard to show people how much I loved them in my language, and they didn't recognize it! The first time I read the book, I just cried. I realized that I had tried hard to make some people love me, but they did already.

Positive Personality Profiles: D-I-S-C-over Personality Insights to Understand Yourself and Others! by Dr. Robert Rohm helped me to realize that we are all wired differently. We process things individually, and some may respond differently from the way I do. It helped me understand more of what motivates a person so that I can relate to them more effectively. I also learned that even though we are primarily one of the four personality profiles, when we are under stress, we will often go to another personality quadrant! It was incredibly freeing to me to realize that.

I also like Laugh Your Way To A Better Marriage by Mark Gungor. We have the 4-disc DVD set of this. It's such useful information that we have hosted five or six different showings with groups of friends (one group at a church had 40 people show up!)

True story on the last one I'll mention: How To Win Friends and Influence People by Dale Carnegie. Years ago, I got into business with some other successful business owners. They were the first to show me some of these books on communication skills, understanding love languages, and different personalities. I was a sponge for this information! I loved discovering these things and knew there was so much I needed to learn!

One day, I got to meet with Steve and Kathy Edwards, good friends, and business mentors of mine. I said, "Hey, Steve! With where I'm at in my personal growth and the growth of my business right now, what book would you recommend I read next?" Without a moment's hesitation, he said, "How To Win Friends and Influence People by Dale Carnegie." I said, "Oh, I just finished that one!" Steve looked me straight in the eyes and said, "Read it again." Ouch! So guess what, I reread it, only this time I was highlighting and underlining as I went! We still laugh about that every time I run into him after all these years!

Tell me about a difficult commitment you've made, and would you make it again?

When I was blessed with my two sons, I committed to love and protect them to the best of my ability, whatever it took. After 12 years in an abusive and extremely dysfunctional marriage, I found the courage to take both my boys and leave. I knew that if I didn't leave, my kids would learn to become like the example they were watching. Staying had become too dangerous, but leaving was terrifying. Fear of the unknown prevents the right decisions.

I read a story years ago about a prison that played mind games with its prisoners. They would pick a prisoner and blindfold his eyes, take him out in the prison yard and remove the blindfold, where he would discover he faced a firing squad. Then they would tell him to look at the far side of the prison yard wall, where there was a small door. The prisoner had a choice. He could go through that door and face whatever unknown consequence was on the other side. Or, he could just get it over with and choose to die before the firing squad.

The results were the same every time. The prisoners were so afraid of what might be on the other side of that door, of the unknown, that they would choose to die by firing squad. What the prisoner never found out was that freedom was on the other side of that small door.

I had to love my children enough to take the risk to get them out. It was rough and didn't end with a happy ending, but I'd do it again, only smarter. That commitment led to figuring out how to go from being a homeschool mom and a Cub Scout leader to jobs that I could support us with. It led me to a corporate career path. There, I learned many skills that I could later apply to help create and build up Best Cellular.

What character traits do you value most in others?

Honesty and integrity are right up at the top, as it seems to be with most people. Why is that? Is it because it's such a rare thing to find in people and thus very valuable? Lack of those two traits will cause mistrust in a person faster than anything I can think of. If you lie to me once, you'll lie to me again. I respect a person who is big enough to come to me and admit what they did and apologize. That takes courage, another trait I admire. Courage isn't the lack of fear. It's admitting you are afraid, but going for it anyway.

Another trait I admire is a good work ethic (my "Acts of Service" love language talking again). A person who will work steadily, even when no one is looking, exhibits honesty and integrity. Let's be brutally honest. What if you wait until the boss isn't around and sit there scrolling Facebook or messaging your friends rather than doing what the company is paying you to do? Now you're sneaking personal time. Is that being honest or showing integrity?

The same goes for renting a car or a house that belongs to someone else. You signed the agreement saying you will take care of that property. Then you abuse the rental car, revving the engine, and driving it over rough spots while you have it. You would never do that if you owned the vehicle. Or rent a house and trash the carpets and let a leak go unfixed because it's not your house. Would you treat that car or house that way in front of the owner? If not, then why would you do it while they aren't able to watch? Man, I take care of anything I've rented or borrowed better than my own stuff! When I've had to borrow a car, it gets returned full of gas and cleaner than when I acquired it! It goes back to my defining scripture:

"In everything you do, work like you are doing it for the Lord and not for man." - Colossians 3:23

How do you push through your worst times?

I "hang on to my fork." There's an old story about a very elderly lady who was close to dying. Her preacher came by to see her and pray for her. He asked if there were any special things she would like him to say during her memorial service. She asked him to make sure that a fork was placed in her hands when laid to rest in the casket. Understandably surprised, the preacher asked her why. She said that when she was a young girl, and the family would gather for special holidays, her grandmother would gather the dishes after the meal in preparation for serving some fantastic dessert. Grandmother would always instruct them to keep their fork so they could use it for dessert.

The dying woman smiled and said, "I always loved that part of the meal together. Holding on to that fork, I knew that the best was yet to come!" She continued, "So now I know that as I wait to cross over from this life, I have no doubt that the best is yet to come and I want my loved ones who come and pay respects to ask about that fork so you can tell them that their best is still yet to come too." It may sound preachy, but that truly is how I get through the dark times. I know that "this too will pass" and there are better times ahead.

I used to get frustrated with myself when I was having a "downer day." You know, those days when you're just sad, and you really can't justify why? You beat your self up because you know you are so blessed, and so you shouldn't be feeling sad. Inside you are screaming at yourself, "What's your problem? You have no right to be down or sad!" So that just piles on the heaviness and makes you feel even worse!

Years ago, I had a realization. When I

have one of those sad, depressing days, maybe this is one of God's coping mechanisms. That He gives you tears to release pain and sadness, that he gives you sleep to let your brain process life's challenges, that He gives you time to withdraw and be alone with yourself and Him. Instead of beating myself up for having a bad day that I shouldn't be having, I permit myself just to have a really bad day! I realized if I'm sad and depressed, it's okay! By freeing myself of the guilt of having a bad day, that it helps me get to feeling happy faster!

What keeps you awake at night?

Worrying about my boys. How are they doing? Are they happy? Is their career doing well for them? Are they satisfied in their relationships? Do they know how deeply I love them and know I would give my life for them? That's just what moms do, I guess. I wake up thinking about them and pray for them until I fall asleep again.

My son Curtis' Type 1 diabetes is a disease that he has lived with since he was two years old. This was way before Continuous Glucose Monitors. I often couldn't tell if he was just napping or unconscious. If I missed waking up throughout the night, he got too low. I would have to treat him with glucose so he could recover. To this day, God gave me an intuition even though we live miles apart. I wake up through the night and call him until he can get up to test his sugar.

I also worry about our business. Best Cellular is growing and expanding, and I worry about making sure we stay up on industry trends and changes that may affect the decisions we make and the directions we take. We've made commitments to our customers as well as our staff that I take very seriously. I worry about the inevitable pitfalls that throw kinks in the plans. I always remember, "Your word is your worth – and your worth is your word."

What inspires you?

I love learning. I love teaching – kids, dogs, or horses; it doesn't matter. Helping them become the best they can be is my passion. I love connecting and seeing the "aha moments" when you can see the transition. I take pride in helping them "get" something I was trying to communicate. I love training horses, starting as a colt, and earning their trust and respect. That inspires me. I want to help them love to perform at a level that takes kids to state, national, and collegiate championships.

I'm also inspired by being tuned in to a horse or dog and noticing when they are trying to communicate with their human. It could be the smallest things, like a horse showing me where he has an itch and rewarding that communication by scratching him to make it better. Then when I'm asking my horse to turn or gallop or stop or back up, they understand I'm trying to communicate with them as well!

Or my dog trying to tell me his water bowl is empty by sticking his nose in the shower, then raising and looking in the commode, then back at me, and me getting him water along with telling him what a good boy he is for letting me know! Then when I'm asking him to "go get my walking shoes" or "do you want to go walking?" he understands I'm communicating to him and responds! It may sound silly to someone who's never had the privilege of having a horse or dog, but it gives me joy. It inspires me to want to get up earlier and get out there to spend more time with them.

I love a little life lesson I read just the other day. It said: "The words we leave behind will be a lasting picture of who we are." I don't care to have a lot of material things to leave behind. I want to leave behind the relationships that I invested time to build and strengthen, and words. Words of encouragement. Words of praise. Words in prayers. Words in Thank You cards and Thinking of You cards, words in a text to someone, words of wisdom and counsel, and most of all, words of love. Since I help to run Best Cellular, I do my best to use my words to inspire, to build up, and lift our team rather than bark out orders.

How do you manage and prioritize opportunities?

I am always striving to become better at time management and prioritization. It's easy to feel like other people don't have as many demands and constraints on their day. We feel as if we have more to get done with less time! The truth is, we all have 24 hours in our wallet. No exceptions! So it's not a time problem, it's a time management and priority problem. When we say, "I didn't have time," what we meant was, "I didn't make that a priority to do in the time I had."

It's certainly true that some of us are more involved and busier than others. However, everyone still has to decide how we are going to spend 24 hours every day. That requires each of us to put a priority on the list. How many hours do we waste in front of the television, or scrolling through social media? You'd probably be amazed at how much more time you have to get the essential things done if you unplugged the TV and turned off your phone!

I'm also learning to delegate and to trust my team. Of course, that's after investing enough time to enable competency. That allows me to tackle other projects that need attention.

What advice would you give to your 18-year-old self?

I would say, "Hey, everyone else is just as afraid and insecure as you are at this age! You are liked and respected, and you're going to do just fine!"

I was voted Miss Aztec High School, Class Secretary, and Prom Queen candidate. While setting school track records, competing at State in track and volleyball every year, and participating in Student Council, I was a top competitor in the President's Physical Fitness competition, competed at State rodeo finals, and trained my brother's horse. That same horse took my brother to State and National championships in steer wrestling. I also trained winning racehorses for my Uncle Dave and earned two full-ride scholarships for rodeo and volleyball. I still felt like I was on the outside looking in. Like I didn't fit in or belong!

Man, I wish someone could have helped me with my confidence. I was doing great. I could have enjoyed the journey more! That's another reason I have such a heart for teaching and mentoring young people. I see so much untapped potential. I want them to experience the sheer joy of feeling like they are a winner!

CHAPTER 10

How To Become An "Overnight Success"

Every "overnight success" you can think of has likely gone through years of pain, suffering, delayed gratification, and failures on the road to victory. They are committed. They refuse to give up. People we now see as an "overnight success" probably had friends, family, and acquaintances who saw them struggle and often didn't stand by them. Investing years of hard work and self-discipline paid off, and now everyone says they're an "overnight success."

Becoming an entrepreneur is often a much more difficult task than people think. We've all heard, "it must be nice" when someone sees a beautiful mansion or an extraordinary car.

Are You Cut Out For This?

Don't forget to contemplate the risks, the costs, and the difficulty of becoming an entrepreneur. There's a warning in the Bible about this:

"For which of you, desiring to build a tower, does not first sit down and count the cost, whether he has enough to complete it? Otherwise, when he has laid a foundation and is not able to finish, all who see it begin to mock him, saying, 'This man began to build and was not able to finish.'" - Luke 14:28-30

The fact that you're reading this book is a good sign that you're willing to do what it takes to become successful. You're eager to invest in yourself. You practice delayed gratification. You work harder than anyone around you, often for less than you deserve. Others accept what they're offered. You're passionate about your cause, and your vision drives you.

Many are easily inspired but forget to consider the cost of success. Years of financial losses, stress, bouts of poverty, 6-7 day work weeks, and sleepless nights may lie ahead. Those with "real jobs" are home relaxing on the weekends. Are you willing to do what it takes to become successful?

People often don't want to risk switching products or services until they know the provider has a proven track record. Many of your friends, relatives, and neighbors may not support you or your business until it's already successful. You can't blame them. None of us likes change! Don't let it hurt your feelings when those close to you aren't comfortable supporting you yet. Use that as motivation to succeed!

Damaged Relationships

You may have a spouse or significant other who isn't willing to go through the struggles required to build your empire. They may get frustrated when you don't have time to do weekly date nights or family outings that people with typical 9 to 5 jobs enjoy. You might lose friends because you don't have time to go out every Friday night. Are you okay with that?

For the first few years, you may likely work for lower wages than many of your employees. You probably won't enjoy the vacations and perks that you would have if you worked at a regular job. Are you willing to sacrifice today's "easy life" to build an empire that can provide an incredible lifestyle?

I know multiple entrepreneurs who ended up living in their vehicles or unable to pay rent while they invested everything in building their dream. Many lost virtually everything they had while becoming an "overnight success." Stop financing cars you can't afford and partying Friday nights away at the bar if you want to create a lifestyle that others can only imagine.

You've Got What It Takes

You're above average if you count the costs and seek your dreams despite the hardships. Pursue your goals relentlessly. Don't lose focus. One day people will be jealous of how you became an "overnight success."

CHAPTER 11

Make Others Feel Appreciated

I frequently visit a local coffee shop after sunrise mountain biking. Often, I see many of the same people enjoying a coffee, cold drink, or a fruit smoothie. The atmosphere is typically very inviting, and the staff are friendly and always seem happy to see you. I could get a cup of coffee anywhere, but this place has become one of my favorites. It just feels good to be there!

One Poor Experience Can Turn Someone Away For Life

On my last visit to this coffee shop, something was different. The barista who usually greets me with a smile seemed to be having a rough day. As I approached the counter, she kept her back turned and didn't acknowledge that I had entered the coffee shop. The tip jar is usually stuffed with money, but I noticed that this morning there were only a nickel and two pennies at the bottom of the jar.

I waited a good 2-3 minutes, and the barista approached the counter with, "What do you want." It seemed as though my presence was a bother to her. I replied, "I'd like to order a cup of black coffee when you get a minute." I got my coffee to go and headed out the door. As I was leaving, two friendly older gentlemen I often chat with were headed out as well. I overheard one of them say, "That's the last time I'll visit this place! What's another good coffee shop in town?"

This girl usually has a great attitude, and her customers love her. But today, by treating people like they weren't important, this coffee shop likely lost a number of their regulars.

Stand up and Greet People with a Smile

Everyone loves to be acknowledged, even in small ways. Every time a customer enters one of our Best Cellular retail stores, employees stand up, smile, and greet them. What if our employee is on a call or working with someone else? A quick smile and a quiet greeting allow someone to know we'll be happy to help as soon as possible!

One of the best examples of employees making a customer feel welcome is the Cold Stone Creamery in Montrose, Colorado. That ice cream shop is almost always packed with customers, and the employees work hard to keep up with all the orders coming in. Even with a few dozen people in line, every person who walks in the door is greeted by a friendly, enthusiastic voice saying, "Hi, welcome to Cold Stone!"

The environment is so friendly and inviting at that ice cream shop that it's always a memorable experience. We plan to take our employees to see how great it feels to be welcomed with such excitement!

Give Personal Attention

Ask good questions. Instead of "selling" the customer, find out what product or service best fits your clients' needs. Take time to make sure they're delighted. A "good salesman" can make a lot of money closing sales quickly, but someone who makes friends of their clients has customers and referrals for life.

Show Appreciation

Thank your clients for doing business with you. A simple "thank you" goes a long way, but an inexpensive gift or card can also leave a lasting impression. One of the banks we regularly do business with sent me a thank you card that was signed by twelve managers and bank employees. Although we frequently make large deposits with this branch, I never expected this type of appreciation. It made a massive impact on me to know that this branch valued our business enough to buy a card and take the time to have a dozen people thank us in written form.

Listen to Feedback

Most people won't tell you if something is wrong. They simply won't do business with you again. If your customer takes the time to give you feedback or criticism, listen to it! If there's an issue they felt strongly enough to mention, it's something to evaluate and possibly change.

Support Other Entrepreneurs

Millions of Americans own small businesses or classify themselves as entrepreneurs. You probably have many customers who own their own local businesses or sell unique products and services. Other customers have kids who sell girl scout cookies, raffle tickets, chocolate bars or have a lemonade stand. Keep them in mind when you need the services or products they offer, even if the price isn't as low as you could get it somewhere else. If you have customers who own online businesses, support their growth by ordering from their website instead of major online marketplaces. Your clients will feel valued when you turn the tables and become their customers as well.

Show Empathy

Best Cellular has customers nationwide, but when a customer ends up in the hospital or is stuck at home due to injury or sickness, we try to send a card signed by employees from their local store. This act of kindness isn't designed to generate sales, and we don't expect to get any business by doing it, but customers greatly appreciate it when we show empathy in times of need or sadness. We have had customers visit a retail Best Cellular store in tears who mentioned our card was the only recognition they received while being in the hospital. We aren't always able to find out every time a customer is sick or hurt, but when we can show empathy or give encouragement, it often has a profound impact on the recipient.

Making Others Feel Appreciated Is A Long-Term Investment

Ray Kroc, the founder of McDonald's, once said:

"If you work just for money, you'll never make it, but if you love what you're doing and always put the customer first, success will be yours."

To make your customer feel appreciated takes a conscious effort. You have to listen to them, and possibly make some changes to your routine or services in turn. Like many things in business, your work to help your customers will pay off in the long run.

CHAPTER 12

Interview with Paul B. Watson (Downtown Vineyard Church)

I look up to Paul Watson as a friend as well as a leader. He's the kind of guy that makes other men say, "I want to be like him when I grow up." He's great at inspiring others to find their strengths and achieve their personal goals. Paul founded the Downtown Vineyard Church and continues serving as the lead pastor. Paul Watson is also an entrepreneur, a skilled speaker, a life coach, and an author. He's incredibly skilled at surrounding himself with amazing people and teaching others to lead. I feel blessed to call him my friend!

Below are some insights from Paul Watson. Enjoy!

What is your definition of success?

I think that's changed over the years. When I was a younger guy, I would have thought success was tied to leadership or building successful companies (basically being good at whatever you put your hand to). In the past couple of years, my life has had some difficulties. At this point, I think the definition of success at the end of the day is this: do I have good friends, and do I have a great family?

I'm amazed at how many people are successful at work, and they're not successful in their own life. They're successful at business and leadership, yet they are not successful at home. I don't think that success in the world makes a lot of difference if you're not successful with your wife and with your kids. So my best definition of success is this: "Are you winning in the things that matter?" The things that genuinely matter are family and friends. That would be my definition of success.

When did you consider yourself a success?

That's a pretty interesting question because when I was young, I didn't see myself as a leader. As an adult, I can see myself on the playground rounding up all the other kids, and I was always the kid picking teams. I was never the kid on the wall. When I got into high school, I was the person who made things happen.

I really didn't know that I was a leader until I was in my early 20's when I took the Myers-Briggs test. When it was all said and done, the Myers-Briggs test indicated that I should do something centered around leadership. It had on there, "pastor a church," even though at that time I was on probation. Yeah, I was on probation for three and a half years for some shenanigans I did. So, I took this test, and the test said I should pastor a church, lead a corporation, or go to leadership school. But I didn't realize I was a leader until I was about 21 or 22 years of age.

I used to think you measured yourself as a success by what you'd write on a book jacket. If I were writing a book about myself, I could say I'm an author, a public speaker, church planter, business owner, etc. All of those would look good on a jacket. Then what I found was that, truthfully, all those things that look good on a book jacket don't mean a thing.

I consider myself a success if, at the end of the day, my wife and kids love me. I've got a fantastic family, and I'm very close to my wife and kids. If I'm successful there, then I'm good. There was a point in time when I was not successful in that area of my life. I was successful everyplace else. I could walk down the street, and a lot of people called my name, but my kids didn't want to be around me. So I worked hard at that. I now have a very close family.

The most important people in my life are my family and some close friends. If I'm winning in that ball-field, then I could care less if I'm a corporate CEO (although I am a corporate CEO of sorts). We pastor a great church in Grand Junction, and at the end of the day, that's nice, but I would never consider myself a success in that sense.

We've started some cool projects. Many years ago, I started a camp that now hosts 1,000 kids a year from five states. It's called "White Out." That's successful. We started a program called "The Good Samaritan Clinic," which is a privately funded medical clinic in Grand Junction. People get to see doctors, and it doesn't cost them a dime. That's successful. The church is a success. I've had a business that did really well. All of those are charming stories for book covers and jackets. What really matters is this: my kids are grown, and we're still very close. One's married, one's getting married and they come over every Sunday for dinner at 6:00. That's my favorite meeting of the week!

What steps do you take daily to improve?

- I'm a devotion guy. I try to do my devotions daily. That means I read my Bible. I pray every day.
- I think you have to put things on your calendar. Some people would call them "stretch goals." You have to put something on your schedule to make sure you're improving.
- I listen to audiobooks a lot. I read books a lot.
- Curtis and I both have a little project we're working on this year. We're each trying to ride our bike for 100 days. Neither one of us have ever done that, but both of us are going to accomplish it. He's going to achieve it before me!

"Practicing what you preach" has become vital to me over the last couple of years. I had taught leadership for many, many years. I trained and hosted conferences for many years. I knew what to tell people, but that didn't mean I was doing what I told them to do. There's a big difference between knowing and doing. So I stopped teaching leadership conferences at the time because I wasn't doing what I told people they should do. I just started the conferences again this year.

When you're not in pain, it's easy to know what to do. But when you go through hard times or take a downturn, and have to lay everyone off or fire people, those things become much more challenging. So now, I work hard at making sure that I'm doing what I say. I think improvement comes when you do what you say you're going to' do.

What have you recognized as your greatest strengths, and how have they impacted your success?

The thing that I used to think of as my greatest strength was leadership. Truthfully, the greatest strength that I find in myself at this current phase of my life would be trying to practice loyalty. I'm also working hard at not getting offended but instead having thicker skin. We think of leaders as being great at leadership, excellent at decision-making, and skilled at hiring and firing people. I think all of that is true. Those are really great leadership characteristics. I've tried to grow in those areas.

If you want to be a leader, here's what that means: you're going to take shots that other people don't, and if you don't prepare yourself for that, those shots will eventually take you out. As I said earlier, it's been a tough road and very painful. For a while, I got offended, and I got my feelings hurt when people I loved walked away. So, my greatest strength that I'm working on these days is not being offended and holding people loosely.

I try to be thankful for everyone that's been on the team whether they've come or they've gone. Several years ago, I was at a leadership conference. They were talking to a corporate CEO. They asked, "how do you not get offended?" He answered, "I consider everybody that's ever been on the team alumni." He's saying that when someone leaves the team, we don't consider them a quitter. They aren't betraying the team. They're alumni. What that means is we're thankful for everyone that's been in our lives, we're grateful for everybody that's in our lives now, and we're thankful for everybody in our lives in the future.

Tell me about a weakness or personal character flaw, and what you're doing to overcome it?

I think this is the opposite of what we just talked about. I'm very, very, very competitive. In some ways, that's an excellent characteristic of a leader because it causes you to want to win. But, the problem with competitiveness is when you win, somebody loses. I'm a believer that nobody will allow themselves to lose forever. You can look at somebody when they go through a divorce. When somebody leaves a marriage, many times, they're saying, "I'm not going to put up with losing all the time." They feel like they're always losing in the relationship. The other person walks on them and mistreats them.

So, what I've come to find out is this: being competitive is terrific as long as everybody wins, but when you win at the expense of other people, then it's no longer a good trait, but it's a character flaw. It's a weakness. So, I'm working on that loyalty piece, saying, "How do we all win? How are we all for each other?" The other side is: in leadership; you take enough shots, it's easy to get offended. That's another piece that I'm really working on in my heart. I'm working on not taking offense (unless it's meant to be an offense). People often hurt you, and they don't attempt to, so try not to get offended. That's a tough thing to overcome. Don't take offense, unless it's meant to be offensive!

How do you make important decisions?

Oh my gosh! I am the worst decision-maker in the world! When I was young, I was on probation for some stuff I did. I was on probation for three and a half years. When others were saying something was a bad idea, I would be thinking, "What a great idea!" I would find myself making bad decisions, and then I would get arrested. I think I've been in the back of a police car at least twenty times with handcuffs. Not for many years since, but as a kid, I was in the back of a police car a lot. What I realized is that I was a bad decision-maker.

Now I do two things: If I think it's the right decision, I don't go with my first instinct, and I give myself time to process. I ask two or three people what they think. It's not that I don't make impulsive decisions. I've taught myself not to act on my first instinct because that initial instinct isn't very good. This little thing that I've learned has served me well. I have good instincts when it comes to business, leadership, and growing things. But I can also get myself into trouble. So whenever there's an impulsive decision I'm about to make, I just pull back and wait.

Was there a pivotal moment that set you on the path to where you are now?

Oh, yeah! As a pastor, my pivotal moments are generally spiritual, so I'll just give you a few of them.

The first was when I was eight years of age. I had epilepsy, and I had 300-500 seizures a day. I was in a constant seizure. Up until I was about eight years of age, I had petit mal epilepsy. It was heavy enough that in second or third grade, I just wasn't in school. I was at a doctor's office all of the time. My mom used to take me to doctors and faith healers. One day my mother took me to a guy by the name of Dwight Thompson, and he prayed for me. From that point forward, I never had another seizure. So when I was eight years old, I knew that God was real. I just knew that God was real!

When I was 13, I was at a camp, and my friend and I had done some stuff that gets you kicked out of camp. He was going to confess, and I was going to go hide. I found myself sitting around a campfire. I was truly hiding. I was waiting for the head of the camp to come to find me and take me home. This pastor asked everybody around the campfire just to pray about what God would want for them and their life. When I was 13 years of age, I felt the Lord call me into ministry. I didn't give my life to Jesus, but it was very, very powerful, and very clear. From that point on, I never wondered what I was going to do, although I didn't give my life to Christ until later.

At 17 years of age, I was the "popular

kid" in high school. I was doing everything except following the Lord. I kind of had a bucket list of things that I wanted to accomplish in high school, but it all had to do with popularity. I had kind of accomplished that list, and I was in my car and felt the Holy Spirit. I just felt the Lord ask me, "Hey, how's your life goin'?" I was super empty at this time, and I just went, "Not very good!" I just felt the Lord say, "Why don't you give it to Me?" So I gave the Lord my life when I was 17.

Since that point in my life, all the decisions I make are based on my faith. The way that I live my life and the way that I try to love people are based on that moment in that car when I was 17 years old. It has set me on the path so that 30 years later, I'm a pastor. I pastor a really neat church with terrific people in it. We have done some remarkable things, and it all came from giving my life to Christ when I was 17.

Are there any books you've read more than once? Why?

I read nonfiction books. I hardly ever read a fiction book. I've read Lincoln on Leadership, probably a dozen times. The pages are falling out because I've read it so many times. His Excellency, which is about George Washington, is a book I've read four or five times. I love history.

The Power of the Call (a book about ministry) I've read probably a dozen times. I don't read it yearly anymore, but there was a point when I did. The Power of the Call was perhaps one of the most influential books that I've read.

I think I've gone through just about every John Maxwell book at least two or three times. I'm a leadership guy, and I read lots and lots of leadership books.

I read the Bible all the time. As a pastor, I read it for preparation. As a person, I read it for devotion. I read one Psalm every day, and I read one chapter in Proverbs every day. Then I usually read a New Testament book that I'm in. I love reading the gospels. I love the Pentateuch, which is the first five books of the Bible. I love the books of wisdom.

The prophetic books are a little harder for me. They're just hard to go through. I don't know how many times I've been through the Bible, but since I gave my life to Christ, I try to read every day. I don't always read every day, but I try to.

Tell me about a difficult commitment you've made, and would you make it again?

In leadership, there are always commitments. Most of the time, committing is difficult. Many years ago, I was on staff at a church, and it was really a tough season for that church. It was challenging to stay on staff, and I had written my resignation letter. I was going to quit. My wife asked me not to until I get an answer from the Lord. So for three weeks every night, I would take a walk. I'd come home, and she'd say, "Do you have an answer?" I said, "Nope, but if the Lord doesn't give me an answer today, I'm gonna' turn in my resignation letter." And she'd say, "You can't turn in your resignation letter until He gives you an answer."

I walked every night for three weeks by myself. She and I walk a lot together, but I walked these three weeks at night by myself, and I prayed. Finally, she said, "if the Lord doesn't speak to you tonight, you can turn in your resignation letter tomorrow." On that particular night, I was on a walk. He had not spoken to me one time about this topic, and I really sensed the Lord say, "Paul, you can quit if you want to." I felt released to quit, but as the Lord often does, He gave me a followup to that thought.

I sense the Lord in my head and my heart. These thoughts are super clear, and I go, "oh, that was not from me," and that's how I generally hear from the Lord. It was very clear, "Paul, you can quit if you want to..." and then there was this pause. I could tell there was more coming, and the more was, "...but I will still hold you accountable for the call I put on your life."

There are things that the Lord calls us to, where we respond, "I don't wanna' do that." He says, "You don't have to do that, but I'm gonna' hold you responsible for the fact that I called you to it." Jonah was one of those. He could have run from God. He didn't have to go to Nineveh. God made it really clear. God kept putting him on the shores of Nineveh. If he hadn't gone to Nineveh, the Lord would have held him accountable when he got to heaven.

Many years ago, there was a time when I wanted to walk away from the ministry, and He told me that I could. But, "I'm gonna' hold you accountable for the fact that I called you to it." That was a difficult moment, and yet I can't imagine having ever done anything different with my life. The best thing I ever did was never quit!

What character traits do you value most in others?

I can't say that there's one character trait that I value most in others because there are character traits in every human being where I say, "Oh, I love that about you!" So, it's the fact that somebody is entirely given to the character traits that God has given them - that's what I value the most.

You know, my wife is very loyal. I'm so glad she's loyal! I have some fun friends. They are just fun people to be around! They joke, and they're light. I love being around light people! I'm not very light, but I've got a friend that makes jokes all the time. He's very quick on his feet, and he's not easily offended. I love being around those kinds of people.

I also love being around passionate people. I hate being around "doorknobs" (people that just wait for you to turn them to get them to work). I love being around creative people and smart people. What I really don't love the most is people that are trying to be somebody else. You get around people that are authentic and leaning into their gifts; those are the character traits I value the most.

This is about what I value the most, but let me just tell you the characteristics I hate. When somebody invites us to their house for the first time, and we don't really know them, there's this question I ask: "Do they want something from me or for me?" There are so many people who just want something from you. They don't want anything for you. I want to be around people who want things for me. My whole life has been giving myself to people, and I'm good with that. But it's nice to be around people who want something for you, not just from you!

How do you push through your worst times?

The year 2018 has been the hardest year of my life. My father died at the beginning of the year. My mother-in-law died a couple of months ago. My best friend betrayed his wife and our friendship in a horrific way. So, this year I've experienced unbelievable betrayal, but there have been three things that have gotten me through this season.

First, there's a scripture in Psalms that says, "The Lord is close to the broken-hearted." I believe that when you go through hard times, faith is essential. Sensing and knowing God's presence is unbelievably comforting.

The second is my family, my kids, and my wife. They provide unbelievable support. They've been accommodating, and they've been very kind. They've been very encouraging, and they've been very present.

The third has been our church. I really don't know how people go through hard times without a church. I know I'm a pastor, but we received over 300 cards when my mother-in-law passed away. When my dad passed away, dozens upon dozens of people dropped by with meals and said, "We're there for you."

So I believe faith, family, and friends

is how you push through hard times.

What keeps you awake at night?

Problems that I do not have an answer to. Period. I am very self-sufficient. So when I have a staff member looking for an answer I don't have, when I have a financial problem that I don't have an answer to, or when I have a sideways relationship and don't have a solution, that keeps me up at night.

What inspires you?

What inspires me is, I love winning! I love winning organizations, and I love winning Sundays, I love riding my mountain bike to a hill that I've never been able to climb before and getting to the top.

I also love music. I love going to concerts and just energy flowing. I love being around positive people. All of those things are signs of winning. I have been competitive my whole life. I love winning, but winning to me is beyond a scoreboard. You can win in relationships. You can win in friendships. You can win in personal development. If I read 35 books in a year, I feel like I won. If I go down a roller coaster that's going to scare me to death and I get in line anyway, I feel like I won. I love to be on the "W" side of the column. It steals the energy out of me if I'm always on the "L" side of the column.

How do you manage and prioritize opportunities?

I can't say that I manage or prioritize

opportunities. I love creating opportunities. I make as many as I can, but I probably do more than I should. I believe life is filled with possibilities. I look for opportunities all the time, and when I find one, I "dog it" until I get it! I think the difference between leaders and "ordinary people" is that leaders seize opportunities.

Some people see an opportunity, and they'll seize it maybe once or twice a year. I think true leaders see opportunities every day and take them every day. So, I don't manage opportunities very well. I create as many as possible and seize every one I can.

What advice would you give to your 18-year-old self?

"Figure things out faster." I've always been a person that loved to take chances, and I took them fairly quickly. I've always told my kids, "Start a business before you're 30." But I would really like to say, "Start a business before you're 27" or "Start a business before you're 25". Don't be afraid to take risks. Take monster risks. Take them as quickly as you can. Don't wait until you're ready!

The other part would be: "Don't be surprised that good things are going to happen to you." I think that I walked around surprised that good things were happening to me for too long. When my kids tell me something good just happened to them, I say, "Of course it did!" So, what I try to teach my kids is to expect good things to happen to you. Don't be surprised by that! If you're doing good things and you're hanging around with good people and making good decisions, then good things will happen to you! Most people are going through life, waiting for the other shoe to drop. Stop waiting for something terrible to happen! Stop being surprised that good things are going to happen to you!

CHAPTER 13

Six Keys To Building Quality Friendships

Success is useless without relationships. What is a victory, if you don't have a friend to share your celebration? You can have all the toys, fancy cars, beautiful houses, and dream vacations, but without someone to share them with, life can still feel empty. This chapter was inspired by a lesson taught in church by my good friend, Paul Watson. Most of us are looking for quality friendships, and we could benefit from being a better friend! Below are six keys to building quality friendships.

1. Invest Time

Many of us have acquaintances we can call to attend a concert, hit the gym, or invite to a BBQ. How many of those friends will invest the time if there's not something in it for them? If you throw a party with a hundred people, how many of them stick around to clean up once the party ends? (Are you a friend who stays to help?)

If you want quality friendships, you need to invest time. The return is worth the investment! Many people sit around, feeling sorry for themselves when the phone doesn't ring, and no one invites them to do things. If the phone isn't ringing, pick it up and call someone! Make an effort and be the friend who invites others.

The book of Ruth is a short book in the Bible (only four chapters long) that describes an incredible friendship. Ruth showed amazing loyalty when she refused to leave her friend and mother-in-law, Naomi. It starts by telling a story of how famine in the land left Naomi a widow, and later her sons died as well. Ruth vowed to spend the rest of her life as a friend to Naomi.

Ruth 1:16-18 (NASB) But Ruth said, "Do not urge me to leave you or turn back from following you; for where you go, I will go, and where you lodge, I will lodge. Your people shall be my people, and your God, my God. "Where you die, I will die, and there I will be buried. Thus may the LORD do to me, and worse, if anything but death parts you and me." When she saw that she was determined to go with her, she said no more to her.

Ruth declared that she would abandon her people, and her old identity, to stick with Naomi and follow her God. What a testament of friendship and dedication! She chose to stick by Naomi's side and join her lifestyle. Tim Ferriss has a famous quote that says, "You are the average of the five people you most associate with." The quality time you spend with friends will make a difference in your life, and theirs as well.

2. Earn Trust

Finding people who are trustworthy is a journey in and of itself. Whether it's personal or professional, everyone values trust, but few people make it a priority. When you take the time to earn someone's trust, you are telling them that you care. Being trustworthy shows that you value their needs, and you're committed to making the relationship work.

Proverbs 20:6 (CEV) There are many who say, "You can trust me!" But can they be trusted?

Many of us have been burned in relationships. After a bad experience, it can be challenging to trust others. Trust is a two-way street. Trust is earned by one side and given by the other. If we are unwilling to commit to trusting others, our relationships fail.

Proverbs 17:17 (NLT) A friend is always loyal, and a brother is born to help in time of need.

Earning trust is difficult. It involves sacrifice, but it can definitely pay off. Ask anyone with a long-term relationship, whether it's a partner in business or romance, and they will confirm that trust is hard but worth the effort. Create trust in relationships by showing time and time again that you are worthy of it!

Three Ways To Earn Trust In Friendships

   a. **Be Reliable.** Whether it's for a boss, a spouse, or a friend, merely showing up on time can make a difference in someone's ability to trust you. Show up 15 minutes early, whether you want to be there or not.
   b. **Be Loyal.** One way to kill trust

quickly is to gossip or talk behind someone's back. When a new friend hears you talking negatively about someone who isn't there, it's a great sign that you might do the same to them. Don't say anything about someone that you wouldn't speak directly to them.

c. **Keep Confidences.** A true friend will not betray your confidence. Don't share sensitive information. Treat your handshake as a binding contract. Show by your actions that your word is your worth.

3. Listen With Empathy

A verse in the book of James gives a great example of how to listen effectively. It's also great advice for business and negotiations.

James 1:19 (NLT) You must all be quick to listen, slow to speak, and slow to get angry.

This particular verse lays out three principles for listening with empathy:

a. **Be quick to listen.** A crucial aspect of quality communication is the ability to understand what the other person is saying. Don't listen just to plan your response.

b. **Be slow to speak.** Many of us have spoken in haste and instantly regretted it! Take the time to formulate your responses carefully. Make sure you say what you want to communicate.

c. **Be slow to get angry.** Perhaps the most difficult of these is vitally important. While anger might be your natural response to a situation, you have to slow down before reacting. You may not have all of the information, could have misunderstood someone, or they may not have been listening to you! Most of the time, taking a deep breath and clearing the air means you can continue without burning any bridges.

A commitment to careful listening will build up your friends and result in stronger relationships.

4. Accept Their Flaws

Pastor Paul Watson mentioned in a recent sermon, "the best way to lose a friend is to remind them of their flaws."

> Romans 15:7 (NIV) Accept one another, then, just as Christ accepted you, in order to bring praise to God.

Let's face it: no one is perfect. The sooner you accept that reality, the sooner you can start helping others fill in their faults and reinforce their strengths. Whether you're a leader or a coworker, accepting the flaws in others shows a great deal of wisdom. It also helps others to accept your flaws when you show a willingness to work with theirs.

> Proverbs 17:9 (NIV) Whoever would foster love covers over an offense, but whoever repeats the matter separates close

friends.

Dealing with issues and disagreements is an essential part of building friendships. However, we must be careful in our approach not to cause a rift. If you are dealing with a problem, keep it between the relevant parties. Avoid public drama or embarrassment for anyone involved.

5. Celebrate Wins and Share Losses

1 Corinthians 12:26 (RSV) If one member suffers, all suffer together; if one member is honored, all rejoice together.

Celebrating someone's success brings great joy to all members of a team! On the flip side, a defeat in business or personal life can affect everyone around you. When building a friendship, it's essential to understand what each party is going through. When we pump each other up and encourage those who are down, we solidify friendships and foster teamwork. Don't miss the opportunity to rejoice in someone's victory and show them you are happy for their success! Remember to comfort the downhearted, so they can recover and learn how to improve from defeat.

6. Bring Out The Best In Each Other

Proverbs 27:17 (NLT) As iron sharpens iron, so a friend sharpens a friend.

Friends and colleagues have a unique opportunity. As you interact with those around you, remember that your actions have farther-reaching consequences than you will ever know. Alongside this responsibility comes an exciting prospect: you have the chance to change someone's life! What are you doing to sharpen your friends? How have they sharpened you?

There's a saying, "like attracts like," which means we typically hang around people who have similar interests and habits. Make it a point to encourage your friends and draw them to doing positive things. If your friends are only interested in hanging out and drinking on Friday nights, there's a good chance you'll end up in the same financial boat as them in 5 years.

Dedicate yourself to bring out the best in your friendship. It will deepen your connections, and you will all reap the rewards that come from true intimacy.

CHAPTER 14

Interview with Eric Payne (Venture Advocates)

Eric is a Managing Partner at Venture Advocates. He is one of the leading experts in mergers and acquisitions. Mr. Payne started, grew, and eventually sold Nationwide Valuations, one of the nation's largest business valuation companies. Eric Payne is a skilled franchise consultant and has many years of experience with startup and exit planning.

Besides being extremely skilled in mergers and acquisitions, Eric Payne is also a father, a husband, a closet musician, and a personal friend. He's one of those guys people "just want to be around." Eric always seems to have something fun planned with a group. People always want to see what he's got going on next.

Mr. Payne has self-diagnosed manic ADD, and he's also an adrenaline junkie. You'll often find him upside down on a mountain bike, in a pile of fresh powder, or high-sided on a rock while river rafting.

Below are some insights from Eric Payne. Enjoy!

What is your definition of success?

I don't think of success in terms of dollars and sense (pun intended). Howard Thurman once said something like this,

"Don't ask what the world needs, but ask what makes you come alive because what the world needs is you fully alive."

To me, success means doing things that make me come alive, whether they are profitable and sensible, or not. So I'm about finances, yes, but I'm equally as motivated by family, friends, fun, faith, and some other "F-words" I suppose. I say that tongue-in-cheek. I'll tell you what is not successful to me: blowing out family, friends, fun, and faith to pursue fame and fortune. I'm reminded of a scripture,

Matthew 16:26 (ESV) For what will it profit a man if he gains the whole world and forfeits his soul?

I'm not out to gain the world, but I sure do want to enjoy it.

When did you consider yourself a success?

Funny, when asked about being interviewed for a book on success, I literally laughed out loud. I don't even think in those terms really. I guess it's what I hinted at before. I see success as "having it all together"; all of those F-words in alignment, not one being sacrificed for another. "All systems go." Sure, there must be seasons where we need to be all-in to save our business or save our marriage, but it's not sustainable to put all our eggs in one basket for too long. So when did I consider myself a success? All those values in full alignment? Maybe for a moment, one day, a while back.

What steps do you take daily to improve?

Every year, the first week of January, my wife and I spend a half-day going over our goals from the prior year, celebrate our victories, then set new goals for the new year. We break out goals into Business, Finances, Individual, Family, and Marriage. We review our goals again in July to see if we're on track. Each year I joke with one of my token "Ericisms" by saying, "The goal this year is to suck less than last year." My wife rolls her eyes.

What have you recognized as your greatest strengths, and how have they impacted your success?

I'm comfortable in my own skin (usually). I don't pretend to be someone I'm not. I throw a party to myself every year around my birthday. I'll spare you the backstory, but it's called "The Annual Attempt To Burn The House Down Party". We just had the 6th annual. If you're a dude, you're invited. I love that party. All of my circles show up and cohabitate peacefully together. I have business friends, biking friends, neighbors, poker friends, music friends, church friends, new friends, and old friends. I have no fear of being my complete self at that party in front of all those circles. I'm not trying to keep my crazy neighbor away from my wealthy business friend. Same Eric, take it or leave it.

Tell me about a weakness or personal

character flaw, and what you're doing to overcome it?

I stated before that I'm wildly ADD (Attention Deficit Disorder). I struggle with "shiny thing syndrome" for sure. I tend to be a better starter than a finisher. Knowing that about myself, though, I'm very cognizant that I need to put systems in place and hire my replacement before I get bored, put a wrench in it, and move on the next distraction. Also, being a glowing "D" and super-high "I" (DISC Assessment), I tend to be jerkish as well. So I'm distracted and callous? Good times.

How do you make important decisions?

Oh yes, The 24-Hour Rule. I forgot to mention that I'm also a bit of a postal worker (as in going postal). Suppress, suppress, suppress, everyone dies! So I learned several years ago that if there's heat on a subject, and/or there are long-lasting consequences, simmer before acting. Before sending that next email reply, write it, then stick in it drafts until the next day. Wait to call in that employee until the next day. Wait to buy that new Jeep until the next day. Usually, that email never gets sent, and that Jeep never gets bought!

Was there a pivotal moment that set you on the path to where you are now?

When I was in college, I delivered pizza for Domino's Pizza. I would go to the library and rent 4-5 books on tape (way before Audible). Some would be the motivational Zig Ziglar or Tony Robbins type of books and seminars. But what I loved most was renting autobiographies. I loved hearing the story before their success. I couldn't get enough of hearing about the Lee Iacocca types that sold used cars before turning around all of Chrysler. Those countless hours in uniform (red, white, and blue polyester nonetheless) made me realize that Iacocca's successes started long before we ever heard about him.

Are there any books you've read more than once? Why?

The book that's been on my shelf since college is "The Goal" by Eliyahu M. Goldratt. It's not a sexy book; it's more of a textbook. But it is singly the most impacting book I've read. Although it's a business book about identifying the bottlenecks, process flow, systems, and managing constraints, I see its wisdom play out in so many other realms.

Tell me about a difficult commitment you've made, and would you make it again?

I have a partner that invested in a tech startup with me. He invested basically sight unseen because he's a friend and values my opinions. Over four years, he lost $130k. No personal guarantees. No commitments to pay. But he's getting paid back every dollar and then some. He trusts me even more now than the day we spent the money. But you know what else? He still has money, and he has friends with money.

He's one of my first calls when another 'shiny thing' pops up. There was a study years ago where a company messed up, fessed up, and was extravagant when making it right with the customer. The customer reviews were even better than those customer reviews before the company messed up. I want to be that guy, the one that messes up plenty but has no enemies and only glowing reviews.

What character traits do you value most in others?

Candidly, I carry a massive appreciation that I'm always one poor choice away from losing it all! I wonder if most are? I'm of the age where I'm starting to think about the end game. How do I finish well? Sustain? Leave a legacy? Don't blow out? Another "Ericism" for you: "You don't find steak in trash cans." Also, "You are who you hang with." So, what character trait do I seek out from others? How do I finish well? Hang out with people that are finishing well. Eat steak and stay out of trash cans!

How do you push through your worst times?

Another "Ericism" is "You can't steer a parked car." So I keep driving, hitting bumpers along the way, of course, but I don't stop. Mountain biking is my current sport of choice. Most of my best friends ride. When we teach new riders, we offer all kinds of advice: "Momentum is your friend. Let the bike do what it was meant to do. Look 10 feet ahead, not at your tire." I think the same advice applies to tough times. Don't stop riding. Keep the pace. Do what you were created for. Focus on the future because this season is temporary.

What keeps you awake at night?

Nothing keeps me awake at night. Ever. I can sleep anywhere, anytime. It's a great trait, I suppose. Or maybe I just don't sleep well, so I'm always tired? I should probably look into that!?

What inspires you?

I'm inspired by the fresh and new. I've been called a trailblazer. I suppose I love the thrill of the unknown. Like the bumper sticker says, "Not all who wander are lost." I love family vacations to new places. I love meeting new people. I love riding new trails. I love startups. I love playing music. I love taking risks. I love seeing others take risks.

How do you manage and prioritize opportunities?

This is a weakness. My wife tells me that not all great opportunities have to be my opportunities. "Save some for others," she says. When shiny things create a distraction, and they do a lot, it takes everything in me to stay the course. It is imperative to be in community with other like-minded (and not so like-minded) peers and mentors that can be sounding boards. Slow down. Implement the 24-hour rule (from above). Pray.

Listen.

What advice would you give to your 18-year-old self?

"Eric, dude, seriously bro" (this is how I talk). "Don't make poor long-term choices based on short-term needs. Begin with the end in mind. Prior proper planning prevents poor performance. Live below your means. Seek wise counsel. Pace yourself. Finish well. Friends and family first. Don't hold anything back. Give it all. Be transparent. Forgive and forget. Read more. Pray more. Find out what makes you come alive and do that!"

CHAPTER 15

Meet New Friends

Becoming successful requires hard work, dedication, and a significant amount of time focused on achieving your goals. Meeting new friends can be difficult if you're a workaholic (like many successful entrepreneurs). Below are some ideas that can help you meet quality friends who have similar goals and dreams!

Join A Gym

Exercise is excellent for your health and your attitude. It can also help you meet others who are actively focused on self-improvement. There are many different types of workouts, classes, and fitness groups to fit your style and goals. Whether you find a local group to go biking or join a boxing gym to relieve stress, others are doing the same thing. Take an introductory class or free session, and you might find a friend for life!

Something else to remember: if you're interested in meeting new friends, it's probably not a good idea to wear headphones or earbuds. Hiding out on a stationary bike in the back makes you far less approachable. Don't interrupt someone's workout, but try to keep an open mind when you're in a gym. Greet the front desk staff in a friendly manner. Ask how their day is going. You could be the "bump on a log" who just puts in time on the treadmill or the friendly member that newbies ask for advice. The choice is yours!

Visit A Local Community Hub Or Coworking Space

Many cities and even smaller towns offer community hubs and coworking spaces with high-speed internet access. Search the internet for "coworking spaces near me," and you'll get a comprehensive list of places to work and meet other entrepreneurs in your area! Many of these spaces can be accessed for free with your library card. Most of them offer community events or lectures on a variety of subjects. Go to listen or do a presentation on your expertise. You never know who might show up!

Join A Local Toastmasters Club

Toastmasters is an organization designed to help its members become confident public speakers and influential leaders. They offer a supportive learn-by-doing environment that allows members to accomplish goals at their own pace. Even if you aren't a public speaker, the club provides excellent lessons that can help you grow and improve your communication skills. The people you meet at Toastmasters are looking to develop their skills.

Volunteer

Often, you'll meet incredible people by volunteering. Becoming a volunteer can be an excellent way to meet genuine people and make great friends. A quick internet search can provide a vast number of places to volunteer in your area. Look for religious groups, local clubs, and other community organizations to get involved.

Join A Church Group

Many churches offer small groups to connect members with similar interests. Some groups enjoy working out, baking, playing music, biking, volunteering, community outreach programs, or lots of other activities. Although you may not attend church, you could still make a few calls to see which churches offer groups that might interest you.

Attend Personal Development Seminars

I've met some great people at personal growth seminars, local TED Talks, leadership conferences, and book signings. You might find a great event to attend by searching the internet for "motivational seminars near me." These events offer not only great information and exposure to thought leaders but also a chance to network with like-minded people in your area.

Visit A Real Estate Open House

Look at dream homes in your area. Attend an open house and chat with others who are looking at dream homes. Shake hands. Exchange business cards. Make a friend!

Find A Hobby

I've recently gotten into mountain biking. For the first few rides, I rode by myself, practicing to improve endurance and stamina. After my 50th ride of the year, I joined a class taught by a category one cyclist who competes in more than 20 state and regional races every year. This weekly class improved my biking skills, but I've also met a lot of successful people who enjoy biking! Some of these new friends include surgeons, lawyers, orthodontists, business owners, real estate investors, franchise owners, and other like-minded people. This hobby has led to awesome night-rides, campfire meetings, and fun weekends that I'd have never known existed if I hadn't joined that first mountain biking class.

Ignore Your Phone

This may sound absurd coming from the CEO of a cellphone company, but get off your phone! Smartphones and social media can be great ways to connect and make new friends, but they also make it easy to isolate yourself. Even when you're feeling uncomfortable in a social situation, don't let your smartphone take you away from a fantastic opportunity. If you're in a group of people you don't know, leave your phone in your pocket or purse. Don't start checking Facebook or social media to look important. It sends the message that you want to block others out. Force yourself to smile and go say hi to someone. They'll be glad you did!

Start a Conversation

Often the only barrier between you and connecting to amazing new friends is starting a conversation. Take the first step! People love talking about themselves, so all you need to do is get the ball rolling. You can do this using the FORD method.

- **Family**: For most of us, family members are the closest people in our lives. We have deep feelings about them, and they can impact our decisions. It might seem like "small talk" when you ask someone about their family, but you're really asking them who they are as a person and how they treat their loved ones.
- **Occupation**: This is the go-to for most people, as in "what do you do for a living?" However, you can keep this from becoming a one-note response by commenting on their answer. How do you feel about their occupation? What do you know about that topic, or who do you know in that sphere?
- **Recreation**: Everyone loves to have fun. You will probably meet new friends at a recreational event, which includes a great conversation starter built-in! Find out how long they have been coming to this gym, class, etc. Ask them for tips on how

to improve your experience. You might find a new teacher, or become a teacher yourself!

- **Dreams:** While the other topics listed are great at the beginning of a conversation, dreams dig a little deeper. Once you've established a good rapport, you can look for opportunities to find out what drives someone. It might be a business or personal goal. They could be building the next big tech company or wishing for a better way to explore the ocean's depths. Whatever it is, many people aren't actively pursuing their dreams. If you want to make friends, look for opportunities to help others with their goals. You might create a lifelong relationship in the process!

Use the simple FORD method to strike up a conversation and make new friends!

CHAPTER 16

Interview with Caujuan Mayo (Uprock Publications)

Caujuan Mayo is Owner, Author, and Publisher at Uprock Publications with over 13 books, an audiobook, multiple authors signed. He is the top earner at an MLM tech company. Caujuan Mayo also runs a social media growth company. In 2014 he created Binary Trade Signal [BTS], a successful Binary Options Signal service. He is currently building his brand online and on YouTube. Although Caujuan Mayo spent time in prison, it's inspiring to see the influence he has created since he turned his life around and became a success. Caujuan is easy to pick out of a crowd due to his impeccable sense of style and charismatic presence.

Below are some insights from Caujuan Mayo. Enjoy!

What is your definition of success?

My definition of success is never giving up! I say that because if you're willing to "grind it out until you make it out", then success is inevitable. Never tell yourself what you "can't" do. I always kept an "If you can do it, then I can do it!" attitude about life. If I see you doing something, I feel I can do it as well. If I can't, then the education and answers are only a Google search or YouTube video away.

When did you consider yourself a success?

I considered myself a success the day I was able to walk away from my past 100% and make my money "legit". Never again would I have to look over my shoulder, wondering when or if the door was going to get kicked in. The second time I felt successful was when I made my first $100k from marketing online. It feels good to work from home and make that kind of money. I spend all the time in the world with family, don't miss important moments in life, and set my own work hours. There's nothing like it!

What steps do you take daily to improve?

I try and do to others how I want them to do for me. That's why I put my number out there on everything I market. You will never see me hiding behind a capture page or website with no real way to get in touch. I do my best to answer every call that comes through my phone, no matter the time of day. I also try to outdo myself at every turn. I'm a perfectionist and my own worst critic. I start my day early and end my nights late. I'm usually up no later than 6 or 7 AM, and that's pretty late for me. I find early mornings and late nights are the best time to work.

What have you recognized as your greatest strengths, and how have they impacted your success?

People say "Jack of All Trades, Master of

None," but my life has always been the opposite. I succeed at everything that I put my mind and heart into. I also have a "failure is not an option" attitude when I'm involved in; work or a project. This has been my greatest strength by far.

Tell me about a weakness or personal character flaw, and what you're doing to overcome it?

I would say a character flaw would be not feeling like I could be wrong. I feel like I'm always right (because most of the time I am!), so that makes me think I always have the correct answers even when I don't. That's a weakness I'm working on.

How do you make important decisions?

I make important decisions in a quiet place with only my thoughts and no distractions. I think everything out to a "T" and try to be very calculating.

Was there a pivotal moment that set you on the path to where you are now?

Yes, going to prison and doing time for four years. I knew it wasn't a place for me. I knew I was too intelligent to be wasting away in the land of the forgotten and misfortunate. I told myself sitting in that cold cell that I refused to be a statistic. I would change my life for the better when I got out. Another pivotal moment was when my mother passed away, out of the blue, at 57. It was only three days after her birthday. I came from a single-parent household but always had a strong mother who gave me her best. I always wanted to do the same for her. I hate that I never really got that chance. She's the driving force in my life, and I just want to make her proud.

Are there any books you've read more than once? Why?

Yep, there are quite a few. "Embraced By The Light" is a story about a female that had a near-death experience. She said she went to heaven and came back. I love that book because I believe in stuff like that. Reading that book answered so many questions I've always had about the meaning of life. I highly recommend it.

Tell me about a difficult commitment you've made, and would you make it again?

A difficult commitment I once made was doing wrong for the right reasons. I use to "hustle" when I was younger to help my single mother, brothers, and sister. I did what I had to do to survive and help out. Ultimately I got into a lot of trouble because of it. My commitment was to my family, regardless of the outcome. Even though it was a negative result, yes, I would do it again!

What character traits do you value most in others?

Honesty and loyalty, in that order. If I can't trust you, then I can't be around you. I was taught that if you'd lie, then you'd steal. Both go hand in hand. I have no time for either a liar nor a thief.

How do you push through your worst times?

I stay focused and keeping my eyes on the prize. I try not to let negative energy in. I'm a very positive person and believe in karma, so I try to keep my energy pure. I do my best to refrain from negative thinking. Your words become your reality, so I do my best to speak life.

What keeps you awake at night?

Money! Really though, it does keep me up because my phone is ringing at all hours.

What inspires you?

Money! Seriously, what inspires me is living in abundance without stress and struggles. Yes, I know life isn't perfect. All of us will have to go through our trials and tribulations. But stressing over where the next meal is gonna come from or trading hours for dollars only to still not have enough to make ends meet is no way to live! Being able to take care of myself and my loved ones is what truly inspires me.

How do you manage and prioritize opportunities?

I use a whiteboard and write down all my goals for the day and month. I prioritize and list them. I make a note of the most important things I need to get done. I make deadlines for myself and try to see them through. Most of the time, I push it right to the wire, but I always get it done!

What advice would you give to your 18-year-old self?

I'd say, "work smarter, not harder. There's a better way. Learn everything you can about the internet and start a YouTube channel as soon as it launches. Trust me, you'll thank me later!" I would also tell myself, "The streets ain't it. You're smart enough to create something bigger than you ever imagined or thought possible, but first, you have to focus, put a plan and idea together, and make it happen."

CHAPTER 17

Take Pride In Your Appearance

Dress for the position you wish you had, not the job you have now. When you dress well, it tells others you have your act together. You exude confidence. People pick up on this. In return, they give you respect. Trust goes hand in hand with respect.

When you dress a step above those around you, you'll notice people often mistake you for being in charge, even if you aren't. Sharp-dressed people often receive preferential treatment. When waiting in line, others may offer to let you cut in front. While awaiting assistance, sharp-dressed folks often receive improved service if they are made to wait. When you take pride in your appearance, others feel as if you deserve respect.

Exude Confidence And Control

Dress like the successful person you plan to become. Start dressing and acting like the person you wish to be. Take conscious action to find your style and create the image you want to project. The way you dress and carry yourself broadcasts your personal brand.

Keep Your Outfit Clean

It doesn't matter if you're a doctor, a plumber, a carpenter, a soldier, a personal trainer, or a dog walker. A clean, freshly pressed outfit portrays dignity and indicates you know what you're doing. It doesn't always require extra time or effort on your part. I always hated doing laundry, and as my businesses grew, it became difficult to have the time to do it myself. I started having a laundry service do it weekly. Now I save valuable time, and I can focus on things that make money and things I enjoy.

Get In Shape

We respect people who look like they take care of themselves. When you're lean, toned and in shape, that's a sign that you're willing to invest time and energy into creating the desired results. We don't like to admit it, but athletic individuals often receive preferential treatment over those who are overweight. Besides improving your physical appearance, eating healthy and getting in shape can have a myriad of other positive effects on your health and energy.

Walk Like You've Got Somewhere To Be

Picture if you will, two men walking separately through a mall. The first is strolling, casually gazing. The other is walking briskly in a straight line with his chest out. Who would you presume is headed to meet with mall management about opening a new retail location? Carry yourself with your head held high, focusing on the goal at hand. Move at a brisk pace, like you've got somewhere to go. Walk with authority, and you will be treated with respect.

Get A Haircut

Does your haircut reflect your desired position? A trendy hairstyle or ostentatious facial hair may not always convey the message you wish to portray. Talk to your barber or stylist to find a look that both fits your personality and commands respect.

Stay Humble

You'll notice that taking pride in your appearance commands attention. People treat you differently when you look like someone who deserves respect. Be polite. Stay humble. Remember, when someone offers special treatment or asks if you want to cut in line, your time is no more valuable than theirs. Don't take advantage of someone because they show you respect. This is an area anyone can enhance. Take a few of these steps to improve your appearance and see the difference in how society receives you.

CHAPTER 18

Teach People How To Treat You

Does this sound like you? Your job stinks. You're the butt of all jokes. You're disrespected continuously by your friends and significant other. It doesn't always have to be that way. Learn to teach people how to treat you!

When I was a young man, my mom taught me this valuable lesson.

"You Teach People How To Treat You"

The Associate Editor at Psych Central, Margarita Tartakovsky, M.S. says,

"People learn how to treat you based on what you accept from them."

Here are a few examples where you can teach others to treat you better.

Your Job Stinks

Your boss always takes advantage of you. You run errands on your lunch break. Many of your co-workers don't respect you. You work the shifts no one else will cover and pick up after other's laziness. You've done it for so long you're afraid you'll be in trouble if you stand up for yourself.

About 18 years ago, I worked at a gym that had terrible management. Employees hated working there, and most of the staff did the bare minimum to get through their day.

One day, a toilet broke in the men's locker room, and raw sewage flooded the floor. The janitor (who was overworked and underappreciated) said, "Screw this, I'm out!" and quit his job as the locker room continued to flood.

I was always the guy who would cover other employees' shifts, help fix gym equipment, wash the windows, etc. When something needed to be done, I thought it was my duty to take care of the task, even if that wasn't my job. So, as the bathroom flooded, the manager snapped his fingers at me and yelled, "McCoy! Get a mop and clean that up! You'd better figure out how to shut off the water too!" I obeyed and spent hours doing a job that sucked. When I finished, the manager said, "Hurry up! You've got a lot of sales calls to catch up on!"

Looking back, I realize that I was responsible for the way I people treated me. The other employees at that gym weren't commanded (or even asked) to clean up the mess. Since I never stood up for myself, management knew it was easy to take advantage of me.

My mistake wasn't in being the employee who went above and beyond. You should always try to be the hardest worker.

The mistake I made was allowing someone to snap their fingers at me disrespectfully, then follow their orders. The first time I let that manager snap his fingers at me and tell me what to do, I created a pattern of disrespect.

You're The Butt Of All Jokes

We've all seen someone in a situation where their friends or significant other makes jokes at their expense. Others make fun of their outfit, say they look fat, tease about how they pronounce a word or make snide remarks.

Often, people will criticize you, so they can stay in control. You're the butt of all jokes and made to feel stupid, but when you confront them, they say something along the lines of, "Geeze! What's your problem? I was only kidding! Can't you take a joke?"

If you don't confront the problem, you set the tone for treating you this way. It will get worse as time goes on.

Here's How To Gain Some Respect

Small changes can create a ripple effect and give you more confidence to make even more significant changes in the future.

The Customer Isn't Always Right

Thinking otherwise can result in a severe disservice to you, your employees, and your customers. At Best Cellular, our customer service reps take calls from all over the United States. The majority of all calls are friendly, and the customer is happy to be speaking with a friendly, local customer service rep. Best Cellular employees are expected to treat every customer with dignity and respect, but we never allow our staff to be abused or mistreated.

I've empowered our reps to teach people how to treat them. Best Cellular employees know when someone yells at you on the phone, it's okay to tell them, "That is not okay. Do not use profanity with me. Stop yelling at me, or I will end this call."

Give yourself the right to tell someone when they're treating you poorly. Take action if they don't respect your request.

CHAPTER 19

Don't Let Talent Be Your Handicap

Have you ever felt envious of someone who seems to be good at everything? While discussing finances with a friend, I asked, "How are you always broke?" I know he makes good money, but he often complains about trying to make ends meet. His response opened up a discussion that made both of us reflect on our choices in life.

Why Does Life Seem Easy For Some People?

My friend has always been "a natural." He's one of those guys who never had to study hard to get an "A" on a test. He is tall, and he has an athletic build even when he doesn't work out much. He just has good genetics.

Early in life, success came easily, but he feels that his natural talent can be a curse. He never had to practice self-discipline to succeed. My friend noticed that as he grows older, anything that requires discipline is much harder for him. He failed to develop the skills and building blocks for success, making commitments in adult life a real struggle. He said,

"laziness is a hard habit to break. I developed that laziness of just riding on my natural talent because I didn't have to practice to be good at anything."

In many sports, a "handicap" is given to balance the odds between competitors. For example, two cars in a drag race might be staggered, so the faster car has to recover an extra two seconds to beat his opponent. In real life, natural talent can work just like this handicap. It places you ahead of everyone else in a given area. The problem is that if you start two seconds ahead, you'll never understand what it took to make up those two seconds. You don't need to develop the planning and execution necessary to excel because it comes naturally. Then when you move into an area where your talent is lacking, if you don't have the discipline needed to make it work, you fall on your face.

Natural Talent Can Breed A Lack Of Appreciation

During our discussion, my friend mentioned that another issue with having natural talent is that it can lead to a lack of appreciation. Like the trust-fund baby who has no idea how to manage their inheritance, it's easy for a naturally talented individual to squander their gifts. My friend says that early on, it was difficult not to look down on people who weren't as tall, smart, or naturally athletic as he was. He commented,

"It's hard to appreciate something if you never had to earn it."

We all know a naturally beautiful girl who gains favor on her looks alone. Problems may come when those looks start to fade. If she never developed the discipline to work on her personality or people skills, folks aren't going to stick around. Being a "natural" can be a curse. My friend mentioned that his brother was always envious of his natural talent. When his brother asked why my friend is so good at everything, my friend said:

"I'm not good at it; I just don't have to try."

He told me his brother had become very successful but was never a natural at anything. Because of this, his brother is very methodical at everything he does. He dedicates an incredible amount of time practicing to excel. He appreciates the achievements of others because he knows the value of self-discipline.

Why Is Life So Hard For Some People?

I was never a "natural" myself. In school, I got good grades because I studied tirelessly to be an excellent student. I was diagnosed with Type-1 diabetes when I was 27 months old and didn't grow an inch for two years. I was always the "small kid" until later in high school. I'd have been weaker than the others but did pushups, pullups, and spent all summer working until I could do bodyweight dips to gain strength. Many mornings, I got up early, ran 6.8 miles to school, attended classes, practiced wrestling or football, and ran home. I also volunteered to help neighbors load up their trailers with hay bales so I could gain strength and endurance.

I made varsity in multiple sports and

was selected to compete in wrestling tournaments in multiple states because of my work ethic, not my natural talent. For me, it was difficult not to be jealous of the guys who were natural athletes.

If you weren't born with a lot of natural talent, realize this can be a blessing. You have learned to work hard for your goals. If you want something, devote every ounce of energy. Invest everything you have to succeed, even if it seems out of reach! Create an outstanding work ethic. It will pay off significantly. Being forced to work hard to achieve your goals may have been an enormous blessing!

Natural Talent Doesn't Make You Successful

Some athletes don't have great genetics, but they're still able to become successful in sports because of their sheer work ethic and refusal to accept anything less than perfection. There have been more than twenty NBA players who are 5'9" or shorter.

- Standing 5'9" tall, Isaiah Thomas is currently the shortest player to be included in an All-NBA Team. He is also the shortest player to play in multiple All-Star games. Isaiah Thomas is the shortest player to record a triple-double in a game.
- At only 5'5", Earl Boykins played for a total of ten different NBA teams from 1999-2012.
- Standing only 5'3", Muggsy Bogues played for multiple NBA teams. During

the 1987-1988 season, he played alongside the two tallest NBA players in history. Their difference in height was 28 inches.

Many people with an average IQ become incredibly successful entrepreneurs, not because of their intellect but simply because of their unwillingness to give up. Many college dropouts have built entrepreneurial empires despite their "lack of talent."

I have to work my guts out for every victory, but I realized that was a huge blessing. I learned early on that winning isn't easy. Winning takes work! If you're naturally good at everything, make sure you develop the self-discipline to push yourself to excellence. If you aren't a "natural," don't use that as an excuse to fail, let it create a burning desire for you to succeed!

CHAPTER 20

Stop Wasting Your Life

Many of you know I was given only months to live after being diagnosed with a malignant glioblastoma (brain tumor) in 2010. Doctors at Swedish Medical Center in Denver, Colorado, told my parents to "make the best of what little time we had left together."

Never Stop Chasing Your Dreams

My mom knew that I'm an entrepreneur at heart. I absolutely live for the pursuit of success. At the time of my diagnosis, the doctors gave me 90 days to live. Rather than letting me lay around waiting to die, my mom encouraged me to keep chasing my dreams. She worked alongside me as we built the company that is now Best Cellular.

I didn't die, and now Best Cellular serves customers all over the United States!

Stop Wasting Your Life

We all have an expiration date! Your time is the most valuable thing you have! I'm thankful for every second I have on this earth, but I understand my final destination isn't just being buried in a hole in the ground.

I live every day, with a focus on living life to the fullest. When it's my time to go, I believe I'm going to heaven, but until that day comes, I'll be maximizing every second here on earth!

Don't Let People Waste Your Time

Stop wasting your life. Don't spend too much time around people who aren't living life to the fullest. Choose to be around dreamers. Surround yourself with people who strive for excellence. Pursue greatness!

I don't let people waste my time! Every day I do something to improve myself. I suggest you do the same!

Do You Have A Dream?

Stop being afraid to start and chase it! The opportunities we all have are limitless! My biggest fear is to look back and say, "what if?" Take big risks! Open your mind, and never ever waste your time! Money comes and goes, but you'll never get this time back! We all have seeds of greatness within us. You can change the lives of others around you. Are you taking chances and chasing your dreams?

What Will They Say At Your Funeral?

Here's a quick exercise that can improve the journey you're on. Make a list of positive things you'd like to be known for when you die. Take an honest look at your life, as if you were writing your own eulogy. Write down the great things others could say about you now, then make a list of what you wish they would say. If the two lists don't match, start working on living in a way that matches how you want people to remember you.

On their death bed, many people have similar sentiments. Here are a few common regrets mentioned by those at the end of their life.

- I wish I'd dared to live a life true to myself, not the life others expected of me.
- I wish I hadn't worked so hard.
- I wish I'd have spent more time with my family.
- I wish I'd dared to express my feelings.
- I wish I had stayed in touch with my friends.
- I wish that I had let myself be happier.

Do any of these common regrets resonate with you? What can you do today to make sure you don't say the same things on your deathbed? Stop wasting your life on things that don't matter!

CHAPTER 21

The Art of Saying, "No"

Early on while writing this book, I approached hundreds of incredibly successful individuals, many of whom denied my request for an interview. When someone has become incredibly successful, it's often easy to get a big head or make others feel insignificant or unimportant. Below is a reply I received from a successful author, who told me "no." He did it gracefully, without being dismissive but instead leaving me honored. Saying "no" without making someone feel like you rejected them as a person is a valuable skill! We could all learn a thing or two from the reply given by Will Edwards.

Will Edwards, Author of "The 7 Keys to Success"

Will Edwards has mastered the art of saying, "no." This successful author denied my request for an interview but did so in a way that left me feeling valued and respected. I'll include a copy of my email to him, and his reply below to show how tactfully he handled the interaction.

The following is an email I sent to Will Edwards

Mr. Edwards,

I just finished reading your book, "The 7 Keys to Success". I wanted to tell you I thoroughly enjoyed it! I plan to read "The Deepest Desire of Your Heart" next.

I know you're very busy and I completely understand if you don't have time to respond to this email, but I would love to feature you (and your writings) in a book called "Success, Motivation & Inspiration."[1] The book will highlight successful, motivational, and inspirational people like yourself. I'd love to have a chapter about you if you're interested...?

Our Facebook group (linked below) already has 5,500 members[2] and has several successful entrepreneurs and athletes who we're going to feature. I'd love to include your accomplishments and words of wisdom if you have time to do the online interview. (Feel free to include references to your books in the "Short Bio" section).

In the interview section, you can save and continue later. I know you're very busy, so I thought that might make it easier to answer questions as you have the time.

Thanks again, Sir!
M. Curtis McCoy,
Success, Motivation & Inspiration

Here is the courteous reply I received from Mr. Will Edwards

Hi Curtis

Just at the moment, I don't have the time to dedicate myself to writing you a really decent set of answers to your interview questions; and that's what you need for the success of your book. So regretfully, I will have to decline your offer.

However, I do wish you well with your project.

Best wishes,

Will :)

Will Edwards is an author who has numerous books published about Self-Help, Business, and Spirituality. Of course, he likely has an incredibly busy schedule. Still, he took the time to reply in a manner that made it sound like my project was important. He expressed that he was afraid he wouldn't be able to dedicate the time necessary for him to create a good enough response. Very classy!

People are drawn to success. I mentioned in an earlier chapter that people would contact you as you achieve your goals, looking to associate with your accomplishments. If you have to turn someone down, turn them down politely. Don't burn bridges, but follow the example set by this author who turned me down early on, without being rude. Even when

saying "no," you can still motivate and
inspire others!

CHAPTER 22

Interview with Nathan Schulhof (Father of the MP3 Player)

Nathan M. Schulhof is a visionary entrepreneur who was a key player at the beginning of the technology era. Mr. Schulhof is the lead inventor on three U.S. patents, and he is also listed or referenced in numerous other patents.

Nathan's book, "Father of the MP3 Player: Lessons in Business and Life from a Visionary Entrepreneur", is available on Amazon, Booktopia, GoodReads, and numerous other publishers. He was featured in Gizmodo.com, Wired.com, Men's Health – Top 100 Tech Guide, Cult of Mac, Wall St Journal & other technology and business publications. He has received numerous awards, such as an Innovations Award from the Consumer Electronics Show, and the People's Choice award from Upside Magazine.

Nathan Schulhof has worked with and consulted for Apple since 1980. If you own a portable media player or a smartphone, chances are you own a product today that uses the technology invented by Nathan Schulhof.

Schulhof is involved in creating green energy and other emerging technologies. He also founded Future Technology Corporation, which produces low wattage power systems for developing nations. Most recently, he has focused on developing fuel cells and power systems for these countries as well!

Today, Mr. Schulhof is a board member of

several companies and continues to consult with them. He is also a keynote speaker at events around the world, where he enlightens his audiences about the future of these technologies, and how to use them to lead a better and healthier life.

Below are some insights from Nathan Schulhof. Enjoy!

What is your definition of success?

My definition of success has evolved over the years. For most of my life, success was about achieving wealth and possessions. I lived for "the future". Today I am a comfortable minimalist. I still like nice things, but I try to live in the present. My goal is to achieve tranquility and peace of mind. I try not to accumulate possessions and only keep items I use at least every month or week. I have always been a happy person, but I have found one can be happy and mentally tortured at the same time. It's important to remember that at the end of the day, we are all renters.

When did you consider yourself a success?

In 1980 I started my first company called Silicon Valley Systems. We made a best-selling word processor for early Apple Computers. Our product, "Word Handler" (the word processor) and "List Handler" (an early relational database), cost $3.63 to produce. We sold it to computer stores for $149, with a retail price of $249. We were all young and dumb, but despite ourselves, we made lots of money. At 32, I was "the old man." This was my first real success. That gave me confidence, which led to other achievements.

What steps do you take daily to improve?

When I was building my company, I understood that to become successful; I had to be at my peak performance every day. I ran five miles, six days per week. I ate extremely healthy and was light on alcohol. My passion and complete commitment were an essential part of my success. I also meditated daily to keep my mind at peak performance.

What have you recognized as your greatest strengths, and how have they impacted your success?

My greatest strengths are my passion, commitment, and belief in what I'm doing. When I was in my twenties, I tried selling insurance for New York Life because I scored so high on their aptitude test. I didn't even try to stay longer than a year because I didn't believe in it, and I wasn't committed. However, the president of New York Life came on my Board of Directors at Audio Highway out of that experience.

Tell me about a weakness or personal character flaw, and what you're doing to overcome it?

As an entrepreneur, I have been too early with some of my product ideas, including the MP3 Player, because the internet base was too small at the time and needed to grow to attract tier-1 content.

How do you make important decisions?

One technique I have used for years I referred to as "The Spock Technique". I would find I made my best decisions when I could keep all emotions out of the equation. I would close my eyes and meditate and become one with Mr. Spock, a Vulcan who has no emotions. I would become Mr. Spock and make the decision he would make. I also like to research the facts and hear opinions from trusted advisors. It's essential to look at all possible outcomes (as you would when making financial projections).

Was there a pivotal moment that set you on the path to where you are now?

Financially, it would be when Audio Highway went public in December 1998. I had another personal growth moment on January 16, 2004, when I went into a coma from an untreated toothache. My body went septic, and I had an 8-year recovery. This gave me a new appreciation for life. Also, producing the first major cybercast at Dodger Stadium, Wango Tango, which was covered by Entertainment Tonight.

Are there any books you've read more than once? Why?

"As a Man Thinketh" by James Allan and, of course, "Father of the MP3 Player: Lessons in Business and Life" by Nathan Schulhof and John Seeley.

Tell me about a difficult commitment you've made, and would you make it again?

Starting Silicon Valley Systems, TestDrive, and Audio Highway were all difficult commitments.

What character traits do you value most in others?

Passion and loyalty to your committed cause.

How do you push through your worst times?

I push through tough times with exercise, proper nutrition, meditation, and logic.

What keeps you awake at night?

For most of my life, I have only slept four hours per night. I have not been able to turn off my mind at night.

What inspires you?

1. Things that haven't been done before.
2. The future.
3. When someone says, "you can't do that".

How do you manage and prioritize opportunities?

Usually, I prioritize by profit and loss. In the past, I said, "a company runs on sales and collections." There are many factors for all that to happen. Today, I prioritize by lifestyle and lack of stress.

What advice would you give to your 18-year-old self?

In 2017, I gave a Keynote speech in Guadalajara, Mexico, to 25,000 young adults attending the conference. After the keynote in a media interview, a reporter asked me to give a piece of advice. Here was my recommendation: "When you have passion in your heart, stay with it. Don't let doubtful people discourage you. Make smart decisions, but if you believe in your plan, stick with it!"

CHAPTER 23

Does Using Profanity Make You Seem More Successful?

It's challenging to have an unbiased opinion on this topic. My goal isn't to convince you, but instead, share both arguments and let you decide.

Is Swearing a Sign of Intelligence?

If a hundred public speakers give a similar speech, but one guy is yelling profanity, you may be offended, but you'll remember the guy who's swearing. I've seen studies quoted that say cussing is a sign of intelligence.

Although I don't relate to his use of profanity, Gary Vaynerchuk (known by millions as "Gary Vee") has created one of the most influential personal brands in the industry. Gary Vaynerchuk provides incredible advice and insights for young entrepreneurs. Still, many were unable to connect because of his frequent use of obscenity.

Curse Free GaryVee

In April 2019, I reached out to Gary about his use of profanity, and I'm sure others had as well. He's been an early adapter in dozens of platforms, and it was great to see that he launched Curse Free GaryVee to provide censored content to subscribers who wanted to gain from his wisdom, without compromising their values.

Gary didn't pretend he doesn't curse in real life, or act inauthentic, and it takes a lot of additional work to create censored versions of his talks. Curse Free GaryVee provides content that's relatable to a wider audience, while he continues to produce the uncensored versions for other fans.

Does Cussing Make You Smarter?

If you have never said a cuss word but decide to try swearing, does your IQ automatically increase? What if you're a brain surgeon who swears like a sailor? Do you lose your intelligence if you decide to stop using profanity?

Do People Who Refuse To Curse Have Stronger Willpower?

I decided a few years back to intentionally remove myself from negative situations and distance myself from negative people. In June of 2012, I decided to make a serious effort to remove cursing from my vocabulary.

I can tell you from experience; this was not an easy decision. It has taken a great deal of courage at times.

Stopping swearing didn't make me less intelligent, but it did make me more relatable. In a group that uses profanity, I wouldn't be excluded if I chose not to swear. In most professional situations, if I incorporated the "f-bomb," I'd probably make someone uncomfortable or unwilling to do business with me.

How Do I Want To Influence Others?

Gallant Dill commented on how the world is a rough place, and profanity is used everywhere. He mentioned that it's a lie to protect your kids from swearing. He said they'll hear it when they're away from you anyways.

If You Don't Cuss In Front Of Your Children, Does That Make You A Liar?

Does keeping your kids from profanity hide them from the harsh reality of the "real world"? Kayla Hutton said this about the use of profanity in front of kids.

"Why do parents need to be the 'harsh reality'? For example: Just because there are drug addicts and alcoholics in the world, that doesn't mean we need to be the bad influence our kids will see, right?"

Does Using Profanity Make Me Seem More Influential?

What if I said the "F-word" right now? Does that automatically make you think I'm more successful, smarter, or more influential? Would it increase my IQ or make me look stronger to you?

We Become What We Surround Ourselves With

A few years back, I was on a second date. We went to see a new movie release that premiered that evening. The theater was packed. We started snacking on buttery popcorn and chatting quietly until the movie started. The previews finished, and the movie began. Suddenly, there was a long string of vulgar words, and the star of the film used the Lord's Name in vain.

I stood up, grabbed my jacket, and told my date I wasn't going to stay for the movie. I was nervous not only about what she would think but also because we were in front of an absolutely packed theater. She was frustrated and embarrassed that I decided to walk out in front of the whole theater. She told me, "It's just words!" trying to convince me to continue watching.

I expected harsh judgment from other moviegoers (especially as my date chastised me). Then a guy in the back started slow-clapping. As I tried to slip out quietly, other people joined the clapping. Soon a number of them stood up and left the theater with me!

That first guy who clapped loudly gave others the courage to join in. They stood up to remove themselves from a situation where they weren't comfortable with the profanity.

I wish I knew who the guy was because I'd love to thank him. In my date's eyes, he transformed me from looking like a weakling who couldn't stand a few vulgar words, to a leader who started a mini-revolution at the local movie theater.

Is The "Poverty-Of-Vocabulary" (POV)

Hypothesis True?

The POV hypothesis states that people who swear regularly have a limited vocabulary. This theory suggests that people who swear are less intelligent because they don't know other non-offensive words.

I don't think the use of profanity has much to do with your lack or abundance of vocabulary but instead correlates more closely with a person's willpower.

I read or listen to an average of 6.4 books per month. As I learn and grow, my views and understanding of life change.

Does Cussing Make People Respect You More?

I don't automatically think you're an idiot if you use profanity in conversation. Still, I do respect those who choose non-vulgar communication when a cuss-word may have been the natural response.

If you watched two guys accidentally smash their finger with a hammer, who would you respect more?

1. Guy number one smashes his finger, then throws the hammer, kicks a bucket over, and screams a string of cuss words that would make a sailor blush.
2. Guy number two smashes his finger and jumps up and yells, "WOW THAT HURT!!!" Painfully grimacing, jaw clenched, and sucking air through his teeth, he paces back and forth. You

never hear him swear.

Who do you respect more in that situation?

CHAPTER 24

Improve Your Attitude

Improve your attitude, and you can determine your success. Behavior reflects thought patterns. Learn to control your mind, and you can set your actions on the course you desire. This chapter includes a few ways to improve your attitude to accomplish your goals.

Be Thankful

Here are just a few ideas on how to develop a thankful mindset:

- **Create A Gratitude Journal.** Sit down and write out some things you can be thankful for, including the most obvious ones. Include both big blessings and little joys. This simple exercise forces you to reflect on your day, your month, or even your entire life. You might discover some things that you always took for granted! You can keep a regular "gratitude journal" to track blessings in life and refer to these good things when times seem dark.
- **Speak Your Appreciation.** Don't let a busy schedule keep you from expressing gratitude to others. Even if you only have time for a quick "thank you", it can have a lasting impact. A cheery, thankful attitude is contagious. You never know how much a simple phrase can improve

158

someone's day. For friends and coworkers, a note or voicemail telling them how awesome they are and how much you appreciate them can mean a lot. Be sure to include why their actions mean so much to you and don't wait for a "special occasion". Everyone loves a pleasant surprise!

- **Change Your Perspective.** When you're facing a difficulty or challenge, stop and ask yourself, "what good can come of this situation?" If you focus on what you can learn from struggles instead of sinking into negative feelings, you will turn those experiences into valuable lessons.
- **Choose Thankful Language.** Your words have power, and they will affect your attitude. Decide to express gratitude in the face of your stress, and it will, in turn, drive your thoughts to a more thankful place.
- **Give Thanks.** I often enjoy giving thanks to God for the good things that are happening in my life. I know God is not a magic genie who can be tricked into giving me more because I said thanks for previous gifts. I give thanks simply because I'm grateful for the blessings I've already received. My appreciation grows once I've given thanks.

Being thankful is the easiest way to improve your attitude. Start today!

Be Motivated And Passionate

Successful people stand out in a crowd

because they are passionate about what they do. The momentum of your drive can often create a "ripple effect", sometimes for generations. However, others may ridicule you as a "dreamer" because they don't understand your vision. Don't let that discourage you! You might be creating something in a new space that no one understands yet. Remember that not everyone was meant to be you or chase your dreams. Passion is infectious, especially when coupled with results. Keep working to pursue your goals, and others will soon follow.

Be Bold

Many successful entrepreneurs are bold and charismatic. They are unafraid to sail out into uncharted waters looking for the treasures of success. The word "entrepreneur" itself means "a person who organizes and operates a business or businesses, taking on greater than normal financial risks to do so." As author Ralph Waldo Emerson once said,

"Do not go where the path may lead, go instead where there is no path and leave a trail."

While you don't have to be the center of attention everywhere you go, have faith in your abilities and the importance of your mission. Write down why you are pursuing your goals so you can remind yourself often. Confidence in your purpose will help you stick with it and inspire others along the way.

You may be going places and creating

things that no one else has before. Don't wait for permission to blaze a new trail! It's best to weigh the risks and rewards, but never allow the fear of unknown territory to prevent you from accomplishing great things.

Be Flexible, And Willing To Adapt

Adaptability is like a super-power. It can take an entrepreneur from "zero to hero" status. Roll with the punches and pivot to new strategies when necessary. People will desert you. Circumstances will change. Plans will fail. That's the reality! New people may join your cause along the way! Plan to accommodate downturns. Ready yourself to shift your focus when necessary. Genius mathematician, Albert Einstein, used flexibility to define mental capacity:

> "The measure of intelligence is the ability to change."

Another way to enhance your adaptability is to define your purpose. Establish that "center of gravity" so you can keep the proper perspective amid fluctuating circumstances. Nail down the most important thing early on. A lot of what you fuss over isn't making an impact on your future. Learn to drop the fluff without losing what is essential. Flexibility in the face of adversity can be the difference between permanent failure or lasting success.

Believe In Yourself

Trusting in your talents and abilities is vital to success. Without the confidence to push forward through failure after failure, Thomas Edison would never have invented the light bulb that worked. His response to all of the failed experiments?

"I have not failed. I've just found 10,000 ways that won't work."

Take stock of your assets so you can make better plans. Never blame others for your failures or setbacks, but take responsibility for your improvement. "Look in the mirror," so to speak, and evaluate your strengths and weaknesses. Find people or systems to shore up your weak spots, and double down on your talents. Always remember that you are the only one who has that unique combination of skills and abilities. Be the best version of yourself!

A Positive Mental Attitude Is Contagious

Improve your attitude, and your lifestyle will follow. Remember that you're not the only one to benefit from this positive change! Whether they're positive or negative, attitudes are contagious. Your friends, coworkers, and family will all see the difference as your attitude improves. They will receive a boost to their own as well. By changing your outlook, you will start a positive "ripple effect" on those around you. You never know how far your improved attitude will go!

CHAPTER 25

Interview with Jeff McGregor (Business Developer, Musician)

Jeff McGregor has achieved success in many areas of his life. After being an insurance agent for six years, he launched an agency in 1989. Jeff and his wife Jan also built or purchased multiple companies over the years.

Jeff McGregor is an expert in business development and also a certified financial advisor. As a spiritual leader, Jeff served as an elder at his church and has a passion for sharing the Gospel.

Jeff is an accomplished drummer who has played in rock, country, and gospel bands. He has performed with Steve Gaines from Lynyrd Skynyrd and bands like Wild Horses. He played with West Yellowstone Philharmonic and Elvin Bishop as well as groups like El Chicano and Leon Russel. After years of successful business ventures, Jeff has retired, traveling the country with his wife, and is now free to resume his music career.

Below are some insights from Jeff McGregor. Enjoy!

What is your definition of success?

I think success comes in many forms, it's not always just financial. There's the spiritual side of things. It has to do with the quality of life and how you can learn from your mistakes. I would say there are successes in the ongoing effort.

When did you consider yourself a success?

That's something I don't think we get to do in this lifetime. I don't have the last say. I try to serve people, and if I can impact their lives in a way that brings them to a better place, or maybe see an improvement in someone else's overall experience, I consider that success and move on. Always take the next challenge. As an entrepreneur, there's always another step to take.

What steps do you take daily to improve?

I try to improve my prayer life, and that feeds into the rest of my life. When you're reading Scripture, God's talking to you. When you're praying, you're talking to God. You just have to keep that in mind and know that it's a two-way conversation. You may not understand what you receive, so you have to be open. I try to look at things from a fresh perspective every day, and I think that's the only thing you can do.

What have you recognized as your greatest strengths, and how have they impacted your success?

Strength comes from overcoming your weakness. In trying to defeat shortcomings in life, you learn how to deal with them better and not make the same mistakes. You still make mistakes. You just have to make new ones so that you can move forward. You have to analyze everything as it comes in and ask yourself, "Is this something I want to be a part of or not, and can I impact it? Can I make it better for someone else through my involvement?"

Tell me about a weakness or personal character flaw, and what you're doing to overcome it?

Judgment is a tough thing for me. You have to make decisions based on what you believe. How do you not judge others in that process? Hopefully, I can overcome that in my life. Sometimes I jump to conclusions through that judgment issue, and I think that's dangerous.

How do you make important decisions?

I pray, and I try to analyze what God's telling me. I don't ever want to misinterpret that. After you come to what you feel like He's telling you, stick your toe in the "water of the Jordan" and see if the water stops. You have to initiate it. Test it. Decide whether you can go forward and make an informed decision about what God's telling you.

Was there a pivotal moment that set you on the path to where you are now?

I think the pivotal moment for me was at a conference in Phoenix with an insurance company. I had just gotten back home, and I got a phone call that my dad had an aneurysm, and he was on life support. I immediately left to go to where he was.

The drive took me about 12 hours, so I had some time to think. At that point, I realized that life was more significant than anything I would experience. We all have to face death at some point and understand that we're here for a certain time, and we don't know what that is. Make the best of it.

We need to try to follow the truth and make sure that's what we're doing. So I guess it was when my father passed. I think that's probably when I just said, "Lord, I know I need you now," and He was there.

Are there any books you've read more than once? Why?

I'm not a big reader (there's another weakness). I tend to get my information verbally. I like to read, but my commitment in time usually won't allow me to focus for that long. So I find myself thinking about something else right in the middle of whatever it is I was trying to absorb. I can take it in doses that are not long. Sometimes that's the way I have to approach it. Audiobooks would probably help, but I just have never gotten on board with that whole setup. I should do that!

Tell me about a difficult commitment you've made, and would you make it again?

I was an elder of the church. I did that for about ten years. It's like painting a target on your back. I think Satan looks at that as a vulnerability.

I would say that making spiritual decisions that affect people's lives is a huge responsibility. You have to keep your interest out of it. You're trying to figure out what's best for them, without interjecting your own opinion. It's a fine line, and it does tax you. My situation turned out to be one that I felt wasn't fruitful in the long run. I hope I had a positive impact on people in their lives, but I don't know if that's what occurred. Some issues within the congregation were difficult.

Would I make that commitment again? That's a good question. I don't know if I would again. I think I decided that I can serve better in other ways. You know, there's a time and a place, and I did my time in that place.

What character traits do you value most in others?

I value honesty, courage, and compassion. I think those are the traits that I look for in people, to see what relationship I can have over time with them.

How do you push through your worst times?

Faith and prayer, that's the only way. You have to have a desire to make it work for everyone involved, no matter what you've taken on. You can't let people down. Knowing that I have that responsibility and that I have an obligation to the Lord, that's important to me.

What keeps you awake at night?

Not much keeps me awake at night. I try not to do anything that would make me stay up because I didn't deal with it. Take care of problems as they arise.

What inspires you?

I'm inspired the most by the sacrifice of those who go into the military. It takes someone willing to invest who they are and what they are. They put it on the line for everyone else. It's an incredible thing to do.

How do you manage and prioritize opportunities?

I deal with a lot of different issues, sometimes very quickly. If it's a project that I have to prioritize, I will usually evaluate the requirement of my time, my energy, and my ability to impact the situation. Then, I decide which ones are more important.

I think you pray about those things. All those that aren't opportunities that affect who you are, or what you need to do, seem to fall away.

What advice would you give to your 18-year-old self?

When I turned 18, I pulled up to the gate of Caribou Ranch Studios in Nederland, and the gate was wide open (which I've been told was never the case), but I felt like I didn't have enough to offer. I just told myself, "You know what? You're not going in." I decided that I needed to diversify my background to be valuable. I felt like

I had more work to do. You can't finish the house if you don't have enough material.

I don't know if that's a wise decision when you're faced with an opportunity that will change your life, but that's how I dealt with it. I kind of regret it, but it served a purpose. There's always a silver lining to even the wrong decisions. You just have to be willing to look at it from that angle.

CHAPTER 26

Develop Winning Habits

Whether you realize it or not, you have created habits that shape the way you live today. If you created a practice of tithing and saving a percentage of your earnings before spending money on expenses, chances are you have savings ready to invest. If you're in the habit of going to the gym each morning and controlling your portion sizes, you're probably in great shape!

Develop The Habit Of Self-Discipline

What if you aren't practicing good habits right now? Guilty pleasures like overeating, spending money you don't have, and wasting hours watching TV or playing video games can lead to a shorter, less fulfilling life. I'm about to share how to take control of your feelings and overcome your weaknesses!

Studies have shown that it takes anywhere from 18 to 254 days to form a new habit. If you'll push through and stick with a difficult decision, you will develop a practice that's easier to follow.

Wake Up Early

Ninety percent of successful executives wake up by 6 AM before their workday starts. Waking up early gives you time to plan and prioritize your day as well as reduce stress by completing essential tasks early on. I frequently mountain bike at sunrise. On those days, I achieve more because I had time to brainstorm while getting some exercise and fresh air. Start this habit tomorrow morning!

Feed Your Mind

Reading every day is an excellent habit of successful people. You can quickly surround yourself with positive influence and great thinkers through reading. 85% of successful people report that they read over two books per month to educate themselves. Commit to reading for at least 30 minutes a day, and you'll be in the company of the most successful people on the planet!

Be Early

If you're not early, you're late! Be the first one to show up at a meeting, waiting for everyone else to arrive. You'll be relaxed with coffee in hand, organized, and ready to go. You'll notice that you're in more control, and people automatically respect you.

Imagine you're looking to hire a new employee. The interview is scheduled for 9:00 AM. You arrive 5 minutes before the meeting is supposed to start, and the potential new hire is already there, dressed sharply, organized, and waiting. That would leave a lasting impression!

Don't be the last to show up. Everyone is busy, and everyone has things to do.

When you show up late, you're telling everyone else that their time is not as valuable as yours!

Make Time To Think And Focus

Schedule time to think. Whether you create a habit of meditation or set aside time to journal and reflect, it's vitally important to have time to yourself. Your mind needs a chance to decompress and process the day. You can incorporate this in the morning, at night, or even both!

Exercise Regularly

Making exercise a priority will multiply every other habit. A regular exercise schedule will have a significant impact on your success. Even if you're not concerned with making it onto the cover of a fitness magazine, exercise creates momentum so you can power through whatever life throws at you!

Spend Time With People Who Inspire You

We are highly influenced by those we spend the most time with. Recent research suggests that even friends-of-friends can influence your life, whether you know them or not! American author, Wilferd A. Peterson, once stated:

"Walk with the dreamers, the believers, the courageous, the cheerful, the planners, the doers, the successful people with their heads in the clouds and their feet on the ground. Let their spirit ignite a fire within you to leave this world better than when you found it."

Those friends and coworkers you spend time with will affect your future. Decide to surround yourself with achievers.

Make Sure You're Sleeping Enough

Sleep is important! We all know this, but we often sacrifice sleep for an evening out, binge the latest show, or even work late into the night.

Here are just a few reasons why a good night's sleep is critical:

- Short sleep is one of the highest risk factors for obesity.
- Poor sleep interrupts your regular appetite, causing you to eat more than necessary.
- Lack of proper sleep increases your risk of stroke and heart disease.
- 90% of people suffering from depression report a lack of sleep or poor sleep quality.
- Healthy rest increases your concentration and productivity throughout the day.
- Your body's immune system benefits from a good night's sleep.

Make quality sleep a priority!

Organize A Schedule

The easiest way to stop wasting valuable time is to create a schedule and stick to it. Block out an afternoon, get some coffee, and plan out your life. As the old saying goes, "If you fail to plan, you plan to fail!" It doesn't have to be extremely detailed. Remember that circumstances will change, so your schedule doesn't have to be set in stone. Creating an organized calendar gives you freedom. With a plan in hand, you can confidently pursue success! Make planning your schedule a weekly or monthly habit.

The "X" Effect For Starting A Habit

All it takes is 50 days for this strategy. Choose the habit you want to work on first. Then draw a 7-by-7 grid of squares on a card or paper. Cross off each day as you complete your goal. While you progress, you will be exercising your willpower. On the 50th day, you can celebrate and move on to another target. Congratulations, you just created a habit! You can use this approach over and over again to incorporate your desired practices into your lifestyle.

Develop winning habits to set yourself up for guaranteed success!

CHAPTER 27

What Happens When You Become Successful?

I know what it's like to have bank accounts overflowing. I've also experienced having absolutely nothing. I've had bank managers rush out of their offices to greet me by name. I've also endured the embarrassment of not having enough to cover overdraft fees I incurred while paying medical bills.

I often hear people say, "money doesn't make you happy," but I can tell you from personal experience that money gives you options. Money frees you from much of the stress that you would experience without it. However, success also creates predicaments you may not have expected.

What Happens When You Become Successful?

When you hit it big, you'll be surprised at things you hear. Many people will say they "always knew you'd be a huge success," although they ignored your initial ideas. Friends and family who supported your competition instead of your business may come to you asking to borrow money. This year alone, I've had people ask for "loans" ranging from $5,000 up to $80,000.00 with a personal guarantee of, "Come on, man, you know I'm good for it!" Somebody will turn in a résumé when you're hiring after they wrote long-winded hit pieces against you on social media. Be ready for it! Think through your options and opportunities before they overwhelm you so you can guarantee continued success.

People Will Criticize You

I've read numerous articles that criticize famous people like Steve Jobs and Elon Musk. There are over four million results on Google if you search, "Steve Jobs was a jerk." Many people hated Steve Jobs, although he is currently ranked as the world's greatest philanthropist. People say that Steve Jobs secretly gave millions to charity, although others criticized him for not doing enough. If you ask 100 different people what kind of person Steve Jobs was, chances are you'll talk to some who hate him and others who are raving fans, although those with the most biased opinions probably never met him.

If you become a huge success, there will be gossip. On one occasion, I was talking with a random person and mentioned Best Cellular, as I often do in conversation. They shared a shocking rumor about the owner of the company, not knowing they were talking directly to him! Rather than take offense at the gossip, I chose to feel grateful that people were talking about my company. Although we did take steps to stop the untrue rumor, it became a great marketing campaign.

People Will Adore You

Although some people hated Steve Jobs,

others permanently tattooed his face or the Apple logo on themselves to mourn his passing. Talk about having a powerful personal brand! People were so caught up in his success that Steve Jobs had a cult of followers he never met. People often blindly support wealthy entrepreneurs, athletes, musicians, and others who have achieved success. Don't let fans and followers make you overconfident.

Is Money The Root Of All Evil?

When you begin to accumulate wealth, others will often belittle your financial success by using this idea to feel morally superior. Money is NOT the root of all evil, although people often misquote this verse in the Bible:

> "For the love of money is a root of all kinds of evil. Some people, eager for money, have wandered from the faith and pierced themselves with many griefs." - 1 Timothy 6:10

Money empowers you to become more. It gives you choices, and it opens up opportunities. Money allows good people to do lots of great things, or it enables bad people to impact others on a larger scale. Money is a personality enhancer. Ensure you're firmly rooted in your values and ethics before you achieve success, and you can do a lot of good in the world!

Being Successful Affects Your Personality

Becoming successful; financially, or otherwise, affects your personality. Ask anyone who is extremely successful, and they'll tell you it took work. It took a lot of work. You'll need to gain a new perspective on life. In addition, your education, your profession, your partner, and your health are all directly influenced by your finances. Psychologists have found that money dramatically changes how we see the world. If you're already successful, or on the road to success, you'll agree with these statements about your personality.

- You set goals. Your goals are attached to a specific completion date.
- You don't hesitate or waste time. Successful people don't drag their feet. They take advantage of opportunities, even if they're tired, even if it's uncomfortable, and even if they aren't ready yet.
- Successful people typically have positive attitudes. They see the glass as half-full in situations where others see it as half-empty.
- Truly successful people practice restraint and delayed gratification. Successful people don't finance vehicles they can't afford. They don't put nights at the bar on high-interest credit cards.
- Becoming successful requires a clear vision of what you want and the determination to achieve your goals.

Does Money Make Life Easier?

178

Money can't buy happiness, but it can make life easier. Money gives you options, and success creates additional opportunities. Being successful opens doors that aren't accessible when you're earning a typical salary.

Do My Friends Only Like Me For My Money?

One concern I sometimes hear from wealthy people is not knowing whether their friends actually like them, or if they hang around because of the money. I've made a lot of money and had a lot of influence, then lost everything when I was diagnosed with a malignant brain tumor.

At that time, I had hundreds of "friends" saved in my phone. I could send out a group text and have dozens of people show up at a sporting event I sponsored or a concert with free VIP access. However, these same "friends" never called the hospital to see if I was okay when I was given months to live. After Best Cellular started gaining nationwide recognition, some of those same "friends" who abandoned me have recently reached out to see how I've been for all these years.

Many people who become incredibly successful don't have the opportunity to lose everything and gain it all back again. I call it an opportunity because it made me look at who my real friends were and gave me the experience to guard my heart as my business ventures grow.

Romantic Relationships May Change

Many couples experience struggles in their relationship when there's an income gap. Take, for example, a couple who met in their early twenties. He was making good money as a head chef at a fancy restaurant while she was struggling as a recent college graduate. She loved his work ethic, and he appreciated her drive. After school, she got a good job working for a tech company, but she never stopped learning. He continued to work long hours and enjoyed hanging out with the guys. As she continued developing her skills, she earned promotion after promotion and quickly surpassed his income. Soon, she was making more than double what her husband brought in.

She urged him to open a restaurant or take time to study leadership to move up in his job, but he was content with the money he made. As she continued to learn new skills and attend trade shows and seminars, she eventually started her own company. Quickly, the income gap between them had turned into a chasm. As she began receiving invitations to speak at events, she sensed the admiration he once had for her turning into jealousy.

She realized that although they had grown apart, it was her that had changed, not her husband. He was the same guy she fell in love with, but her pursuit of success turned her into someone else. She soon realized that his resentment was not because he was unhappy with her success, but that he felt left behind.

You may find yourself in this situation if you are working to improve, but your loved ones stay unchanged. Look for ways to make them feel significant even though you are paying for dinner or a vacation.

Keep in mind that you can never change others, but you can always improve yourself. Stay focused, but remember that your romantic relationships may need a little extra attention to survive the changes you have in store.

You'll Make New Friends When You Become Successful

On my journey to creating successful companies, my circle of influence began to change as well. I met some remarkable friends who are motivated, inspired, and driven to reach their goals. As I started spending more time around people who intentionally focus on personal development, I made friends who give back to the community. Many of my friends are different from my old ones, not because they drive fancy cars or have expensive hobbies but because they've invested the time and energy to afford them.

They're not comfortable with the status quo. They're always striving to improve. We talk about ideas and opportunities rather than people and events. Early in my journey, I wouldn't have fit in with these friends, even if I had been given the same financial resources. I hadn't yet experienced what it took to be in the position they're in now.

You'll Lose Old Friends

You'll realize that you start to have less in common with your old friends on the road to success. As you begin to acquire wealth, you'll notice that you're able to do things that they either don't find exciting or can't afford to take part in. Success presents options and opportunities that you previously didn't know were available. Keep this in mind: you can protect the relationships and friendships you cherish, but it will take a conscious effort. As I mentioned earlier, becoming successful requires considerable changes in your life. Your priorities must shift if you expect to achieve massive success. You may grow apart from old friends as your lifestyle changes. Remember that they're no less important than you, but it may be harder to relate with them as you grow.

You'll Worry More About Details

People who have always been broke often think being rich is the "easy life." In reality, creating something that generates a substantial income can bring a lot of stress. Successful people often need to focus on the small details behind the scenes that others never need to worry about. Because of this, successful people are often more stressed. Prepare yourself to exchange one set of worries for another, but recognize these changes for the fantastic growth opportunities they represent.

You'll Worry Less About Other Things

There will be difficulties in this life. There will be struggles.

"Getting rich is hard, but being poor was worse. Choose your struggle wisely." - M. Curtis McCoy

Before, you may have worried about merely having the money to put shoes on your kids' feet. When you become successful, you may have to worry about which private school they'll attend as they prepare for a brighter future. Concerns over making minimum payments on-time, covering the cost of food, medical bills, etc. will fade. What you are left with is the choice of how to manage your wealth and influence.

Once you achieve your goals, how will you prevent stagnation? How much of your budget will you allocate to give back or invest in business opportunities? Answer these questions early on so you can be ready for success when it arrives!

"Curtis, because of your lifelong physical challenges, I've watched you work harder than any human being I know, just trying to be"normal", let alone the best contender. I am so proud to see how far you have come and am truly joyful at seeing how far above "average" you have achieved in your life! I may be your mother - but you are my hero." - Connie Wyatt

"Curtis McCoy combines inspiration with down to earth leadership skills to achieve solid results. A must read for anyone looking to better any area of their lives!" - Elizabeth Hamada

"I worked with Curtis for a brief time when he opened his first retail phone store. I learned how to be a proper salesman, professional, and other personable skills from him. He exposed me to app development, computer repairs, and provided me opportunity for the future. It was truly a blessing to be one of his employees!" - Dylan Tomei

"After knowing Curtis for well over a decade, I've come to realize he is a very special young man. He continues to strive forward with new and groundbreaking vision. I look forward to the continued ideas that he will come up with that is far ahead of the pack. I am very proud that he has accomplished great things after battling brain cancer and diabetes. I am also proud to call him my son." - Steve Wyatt

"I have watched Curtis overcome the problems in his life time and again, both with his health and his struggle to build something that will help others and himself. He uses adversity to learn and to grow stronger. His unfailing belief in God helps him overcome the difficulties. I'm proud to call him my grandson." - Flora Bixler

"There are few people that fight for their beliefs with total honesty no matter what life throws at them. Curtis McCoy not only lives by a code of sound principles, he has proven it over and over again with tenacious work ethics and goal orientation. I truly believe in him." - Linda L. Koile

"I came to know Curtis many years ago, when I took a chance on his new business and signed up for cell service. I have never been disappointed. Curtis really understands how to build a business from the ground up and he knows the secret to getting and keeping customers. Best Cellular has the finest customer service of any business this side of the Rockies and Curtis has ensured that his employees all reflect his business acumen. I am a very loyal customer because Curtis has found the secret." - Jeannie Hinyard

"Curtis has used his real life successes and failures to put together this amazing motivational resource. This book was thoughtfully drafted to lead, inspire and encourage others through Curtis's experience and perseverance in life. You are a true success story Curtis McCoy and inspiration to all. Thank you for taking the time to share this invaluable work!" - Jessie Duran

[1] "Success, Motivation & Inspiration" was the working title when I started writing this current book.
[2] At the time, our Facebook group was tiny.

Made in the USA
San Bernardino, CA
16 July 2020